Advan

Procrastination is everywhere, like I
Foster makes clear in this original and thoroughly readable book, it's not
always unjustified. But helping parents and other care-givers understand
why kids engage in it, and what grownups can do to mitigate it, makes
for a terrific addition to the shelf of child-rearing counsel. May we adults
not procrastinate in following it!

Chester E. Finn, Jr., Ph.D.
Senior Fellow, Hoover Institution, Stanford University;
Former U.S. Assistant Secretary of Education;
and President, Thomas B. Fordham Foundation

Most people who are capable of excellence don't realize what's possible
because their procrastination, perfectionism, and fear of failure constantly
get in the way of action and performance. *Not Now, Maybe Later* is a
wonderful resource for parents, teachers, managers, and yourself. Don't
procrastinate another moment and learn various strategies to get the best
out of yourself and others.

Scott Barry Kaufman, Ph.D.
Scientific Director, The Imagination Institute,
University of Pennsylvania

If you have a gifted procrastinator in your family, you'll find him or her
in Dr. Foster's book—along with tips to better understand and motivate
that frustrating child.

Sylvia Rimm, Ph.D.
Psychologist and Author of *Why Bright Kids Get Poor Grades*

Procrastination—the good, the bad, the ugly, the mediocre, and the
positive and negative sides of delaying what parents and teachers may
see as important, but kids may not. Given the multitude of options and
alternatives in our society, is it any wonder that sometimes academics
take a back seat to other activities, and to social media?

And are our kids "driven to drivel" on the internet instead of engaging in "deadline seriousity" regarding their assignments? Joanne Foster
has written a parent-friendly text to help take us into the delaying, and
sometimes delivering mind of the procrastinating child or teen—who just
went to the web or found some other way to put things off because the
Procrastinators Club meeting was postponed. Don't delay—get a copy
ASAP! You will enjoy it!

Mike Shaughnessy, Ph.D.
Editor, *Gifted Education International*

Joanne Foster has done it again! With *Not Now, Maybe Later*, Foster has identified a troubling challenge faced by many families—procrastination—and managed to write about it in a way that informs, amuses, and inspires her readers. From the delightful dedication, and through each of the weighty topics she addresses (including failure, stress, power struggles, and learning problems), Foster uses a light, good-natured tone to provide serious advice and helpful suggestions for parents and teachers.

Not Now, Maybe Later is a parent-friendly approach to understanding an all-too-common dilemma. I heartily recommend it not only to parents, but to others working on understanding and overcoming habits of procrastination.

Dona Matthews, Ph.D.
Award-winning co-author of *Being Smart about Gifted Education*, psychologist, and contributing columnist to *Psychology Today*

A key to approaching a behavioral issue such as procrastination is the understanding that it has different meanings for different individuals. Joanne Foster utilizes this insight, separates deed from doer, and provides a user-friendly and helpful guide to changing behaviors while understanding and affirming the person.

Tom Greenspon, Ph.D.
Psychologist and Author of *Freeing Our Families from Perfectionism*

In her lively, engaging style, Dr. Foster points out that we all procrastinate—some more than others, in different ways, and at different times. This book offers parents and their children positive, practical insights on procrastination, what it feels like, where it comes from, and how to work through it. It's a valuable resource to those challenged by procrastination or just curious about it.

Lannie Kanevsky, Ph.D.
Associate Professor, Simon Fraser University

Joanne Foster has put procrastination in its place! Her fascinating and unique presentation of the myriad causes and solutions of this common habit gives parents all the tools they need to help themselves and their kids overcome it once and for all. This is a book every parent will want to read!

Sarah Chana Radcliffe, M.Ed.,C.Psych.
Author of *The Fear Fix* and *Raise Your Kids without Raising Your Voice*

Time management is a mandatory skill—free will does not mean you choose the assignment, merely your educators. Tragically, few adults ever learn *how* to teach children. Shame and punishment dominate the educational process and reinforce low competency levels. *Not Now, Maybe Later* provides parents the information they need to enjoy success as time management educators and establishes itself as an essential read for human development!

"Mama Marlaine" Marlaine Paulsen Cover
Founder, Parenting 2.0

Once again, Joanne Foster offers compelling insight, compassion, and skill needed to guide and nurture children. *Not Now, Maybe Later* is both a clear and comprehensive guide to understanding procrastinators and a simple and practical how-to manual to help them overcome their challenges and thrive in this fast-paced society. Joanne's sound advice and practical approach make this a must-read for parents and teachers alike. A must-have reference book on every shelf.

Sylvia Kwan
EduVangelist, EDUcational Architect;
Innovation Team, Toronto District School Board.

Joanne Foster is masterful in helping parents, teachers, and students understand procrastination and how it affects not just behaviors, but thoughts and feelings about personal success and self concept. Supported by clinical research, parents and teachers glean practical application strategies on how to use procrastination as a useful, motivational choice and not a debilitating aspect of failure, personally or academically. Dr. Foster has a wonderful way of taking procrastination in our hurried world and turning a potentially negative "way of being" into a positive "way of doing," helping educators and parents work together for the success of all students and children! This book is filled with helpful, proactive strategies for the reader!

Rosemary Callard-Szulgit, Ed.D.
Author of *Perfectionism and Gifted Children*

In an easily readable and engaging format, Dr. Foster explores the reasons why children procrastinate, and offers practical strategies to assist them in managing it effectively. This book offers specific, relatable scenarios and current research from a wide variety of perspectives, making it an essential read for any parent or teacher seeking to understand procrastination.

Craig Phillips
Gifted Program Teacher and Gifted Education Specialist

Joanne Foster has written a parenting book that addresses skills and topics that make good sense for many reasons. Ostensibly for the purpose of teaching children how not to get stuck in patterns of procrastination, she addresses issues related to a child's positive self-concept in general. She describes how to recognize what's behind a particular pattern of procrastination and how to work with the child to overcome it. A great parenting book!

Deborah L. Ruf, Ph.D.
Educational Consultant and High Intelligence Specialist

Children often have their own timelines, which don't match ours, or the busy world in which we live in. *Not Now, Maybe Later* is the latest book from Dr. Joanne Foster, a trusted professional who has vast experience working with both educators and parents. From identifying the many Procrastination Personas, to offering realistic, workable solutions to help your school-age child effectively deal with procrastination, the book guides parents toward understanding why children have difficulty completing tasks. Where the book shines is in the specific recommendations to stage of development (toddlers, early school years, teens, and adolescents) and ability level (special needs, average, bright, and gifted).

A must read, from a strong, reputable expert in the field.

Barb Wiseberg
Editor, *SportsBrain* newsletter, www.sportsbrain.com

Not Now, Maybe Later

Helping Children Overcome Procrastination

Joanne Foster, Ed.D.

Great Potential Press™

Not Now, Maybe Later: Helping Children Overcome Procrastination
Edited by: Jane Hesslein and Jessica Atha
Interior design: The Printed Page
Cover design: Hutchison-Frey

Published by Great Potential Press, Inc.
1325 N. Wilmot Road, Suite 300
Tucson, AZ 85712
www.greatpotentialpress.com

19 18 17 16 15   5 4 3 2 1

At the time of this book's publication, all facts and figures cited are the most current available. All telephone numbers, addresses, and website URLs are accurate and active; all publications, organizations, websites, and other resources exist as described in this book; and all have been verified as of the time this book went to press. The author(s) and Great Potential Press make no warranty or guarantee concerning the information and materials given out by organizations or content found at websites, and we are not responsible for any changes that occur after this book's publication. If you find an error or believe that a resource listed here is not as described, please contact Great Potential Press.
Great Potential Press provides a wide range of authors for speaking events. To find out more, go to www.greatpotentialpress.com/do-you-need-a-speaker, email info@greatpotentialpress.com, or call (520) 777-6161.

Library of Congress Cataloging-in-Publication Data
Foster, Joanne F., 1953-
  Not now, maybe later : helping children overcome procrastination / Joanne
Foster, Ed.D.
    pages cm
  Includes bibliographical references and index.
  ISBN 978-1-935067-26-9 (pbk.) -- ISBN 1-935067-26-5 (pbk.) 1.
Procrastination. 2. Child development. 3. Child rearing. I. Title.
  BF637.P76F67 2015
  179'.8--dc23
                        2013038576

This book is dedicated to my husband Garry who is incredibly supportive and loves me unconditionally, no matter what I do—or when I do it; to our children, Eric, Cheryl, Michele, and Aaron, who constantly inspire us with their conscientiousness and many and varied enthusiasms; to our granddaughter Cara, who often gleefully tells us later and tomorr-no; to little Allie, who has not yet grasped the concept of time, but enjoys playing and reading stories now; and to baby Jake, who arrived early and, so far, enjoys doing things sooner rather than later. Thank you all!

Table of Contents

List of Figures

Acknowledgements

There are several people I'd like to thank for their part in helping me shape *Not Now, Maybe Later* into the book you see here.

Writing, researching, and fine-tuning the manuscript was a major project. I want to thank James Webb, Janet Gore, Jessica Atha, and Jane Hesslein for the time and effort they put forth. The book is stronger for the comments and insights they shared during the editing process. Thanks, too, to Terry, Anne, and the rest of the Great Potential Press team who contributed their energy and know-how to this final product.

Dona Matthews is my esteemed colleague and friend. I greatly appreciate her ongoing encouragement, her wide-ranging expertise, and her unwavering confidence in me. Thank you Dona!

Beverley Slopen has provided me with counsel for several years. She's extremely knowledgeable about the literary world, her advice is always constructive, and I'm grateful for her guidance.

I've had the good fortune of meeting countless parents, teachers, children, teenagers, scholars, and other professionals over the years—while working in the field of gifted education, when consulting in schools and communities, and during the course of writing extensively, presenting at conferences, and teaching in classrooms and at the University of Toronto. I'm thankful to all the individuals who shared stories about their experiences and trusted me to convey them.

This book would not have been possible without the support of my family and friends who graciously showed patience and good humor while I worked on the manuscript (at odd hours, in various places, and often incessantly). To all of you—and especially to Eric, Cheryl, Michele, and Aaron—thank you for being enthusiastic in supporting my efforts.

Garry Foster is my pillar of strength, my best friend, and the love of my life. When my workload gets too heavy or I lose myself in front of the computer, he helps me resurface, keeps me sane and happy, and is thoughtful and wise. Thank you Garry for all that you do, and for helping me to accomplish my goals, now and forever.

Introduction

"One today is worth two tomorrows; never leave that till tomorrow which you can do today."
~ Benjamin Franklin

"Never put off till tomorrow what you can do the day after tomorrow."
~ Mark Twain

These two quotes have very opposite perspectives. Which one sounds like you? Which one reflects your children?

Why do capable people sometimes delay, put things off, or behave in ways that are—or at least appear to be—unproductive? This book is about understanding procrastination, primarily as it affects children, and how to help them overcome it and improve their productivity. Although written mainly for parents, it will also be helpful to teachers and others who work with kids. In fact, many strategies within these pages are applicable to procrastinators of any age.

We see procrastination in many important aspects of life—household tasks, social activities, and school-related and other activities. Procrastination is not just present in behaviors; we also see it in thoughts and feelings about success, failure, responsibility, and, of course, motivation. As you can probably imagine, it took me a while to start this book, and then to finish it, because I procrastinated. It's ironic, but true.

In writing this book, I considered work by psychologists, educators, clinicians, counselors, researchers, and others who have studied procrastination and related tendencies. I also drew upon experiences of those who live with, work with, or are frequent procrastinators, and it became clear to me that people seldom procrastinate because they lack ability. I have worked in the field of gifted education for over 30 years, and I can attest to the fact that just because kids *can* do something does not mean that they *will* do it—or do it in a timely manner.

In hundreds of presentations to parents and teachers as an educator, author, consultant, teacher-trainer, and gifted specialist, I have often been asked what makes some children more capable than others. Much of it stems from which children are more inclined to buckle down and do what is required to become smart. Intelligence is not something that is rigidly set at birth (or at the age of four, or seven, or ten); instead, intelligence develops over time, and building intelligence requires hard work, with little procrastination.[1]

Procrastination comes up again and again as people express concerns about their children, some identified as gifted learners and many not. Why isn't their child or student keeping up? Why does he put off doing homework or other tasks? How can he be motivated? What do you do when a child has a blasé, disrespectful attitude?

When kids are disinclined to do something like schoolwork or chores, whose problem is it anyway? When children avoid or delay, are they trying to be purposefully annoying? Or are they unintentionally exasperating? Does their procrastination indicate something more disturbing? Or is procrastination just laziness and perhaps a normal part of growing up and everyday life, to be expected and endured? So many questions!

As I tried to find answers, I looked at the links between perfectionism and procrastination, and I explored how procrastination connects with other factors such as intellectual abilities, environments, family values, past experiences, self-concepts, and so much more.[2] All the while, I continued to hear questions and sought to answer them in informed and helpful ways. The information-gathering process was fascinating, and it kept me going. *Not Now, Maybe Later* is the result of my efforts, and it is my way of helping people to better understand children's procrastination and to deal with it thoughtfully and effectively. Each chapter in this book has one or more specific areas of focus, and I incorporate discussion, examples, and strategies. In many cases, readers will see targeted follow-up segments with additional suggestions for preventing, managing, or ending procrastination. In all, I provide hundreds of practical ideas for parents and children to use *now*.

When I tell people about *Not Now, Maybe Later*, they inevitably ask me, "Is it for adults, as well?" or "Do you have any tips for me?" I reply, "Yes, I offer lots of strategies you can try, too." And that is really important because when parents continue to learn and work hard, and then demonstrate these attributes, they help their children become more growth-minded and productive. Adults who recognize certain procrastination tendencies in themselves will find many applicable understandings within this book, along with various tips that can be adapted for their use, and then modeled for children. If a parent and child both happen to be procrastinators, they can work on the strategies together, encouraging one another to get things done, and striving toward greater productivity together.

Although procrastination is not always a bad thing, it can lead to stress and be especially incapacitating for children. It can compromise their dreams and self-esteem and result in underachievement. It can be a game changer as they live within their family, move from one grade level to another, and as they mature and develop a sense of self.

I respectfully suggest that you do not procrastinate reading this book.

Joanne Foster, Ed.D.

CHAPTER 1

Is Procrastination a Way of Being or a Way of Doing?

"Destiny is not a matter of chance; it is a matter of choice.
It is not a thing to be waited for; it is a thing to be achieved."
~ William Jennings Bryan

Why would someone put things off? Perhaps he believes that the task is beyond his intelligence.[3] He might think, "I'm not smart enough to do that. I'll never complete it properly." Perhaps a pattern of avoidance has become ingrained since early childhood, and thus is hard to eliminate, like the ten year old who has never had to tidy up his belongings and now is even more averse to straightening up his things. Another boy uses procrastination to challenge adults around him by proudly wearing a well-worn T-shirt that reads *Procrastinators: Leaders of Tomorrow*, and his behaviors follow that credo. Perhaps the opportunity for immediate enjoyment just seems more appealing, and so a teenager says, "I'll do it later. I'd rather watch television." One girl matter-of-factly explained, "In January, I procrastinate because I don't feel like doing stuff right after the holidays, but in May I often avoid my schoolwork because I'm exhausted and just have too many other things to do." However, putting things off may also have to do with logical timing preferences that are quite appropriate. A child may procrastinate because he is gathering relevant information that will allow him to do a task better.

Sometimes I hear parents and teachers say, "Well, he's just a procrastinator," as though that is an inherent character trait. However, the issue of why some people procrastinate may not have to do with a way of *being*, but rather with a way of *doing* that arises from how a person is thinking at a particular point in time. Remember I said I had procrastinated in writing this book? Well, I had a broad timeline for completion so I didn't feel a need to push myself. An open-ended timeline can be a kindly measure that provides ample opportunity to get things done. On the other hand, a broad grace period can also be counterproductive because it allows time for distractions, excuses, and other jobs and occurrences to intercede. When the pressure to produce is off, there's no urgency to begin, or even to continue working on the task, even for an adult who usually is well-organized and responsible. An otherwise responsible child who is given an extended time frame to complete an assignment—say, to write an essay, or research an end-of-unit project, or learn to play a piece of music—may think the same way I did and will delay, justifying this by saying, "What's the hurry? I still have plenty of time. I'll be able to focus more clearly on this later!"

Reasons for Procrastination

Look at the *Why* and *When* Checklist in Figure 1.1. Which ones apply to your children? Have your children also mark the items that seem to fit them. (They can do this with or without you.) When do these tendencies or thoughts usually occur? Is it a particular place, time of day, or time of the week?

Because kids sometimes have trouble verbalizing their thoughts, this checklist activity can help them see patterns in their procrastination. They may also think of other reasons for procrastination to add to the list. There are almost 70 here, but it is open-ended. Each item that gets checked can become a springboard to begin a discussion of workable strategies. By talking candidly through a point without being judgmental and by thinking constructively, you will likely be able to brainstorm some ideas and strategies that will work in the particular context where procrastination occurs. An honest examination of the reason a child procrastinates in doing one or more things is a practical starting point for further discussion. Later in the book, we will talk about some specific suggestions for addressing particular issues—such as low energy levels, a cluttered work space, fear of failure, and other items on the checklist—but an open discussion with the child is a good place to start.

Figure 1.1. Why and When Checklist: Reasons for Procrastinating

Personal Perceptions

○ Looming large – *"Too much, too tough, and too soon. Can't do it."*

○ Boredom – *"There's no point in doing this. It's way too easy, and such a drag."*

○ Tunnel vision – *"This doesn't fit with what I had in mind. I'm not changing my plan."*

○ Imagined results – *"I'm sure it's not going to work out well in the end."*

○ Misinterpretation – *"It makes no sense!"*

○ Nuisance factor – *"This is annoying and just interferes with everything."*

○ Tasks that seem unsuited to timeframe – *"This will take forever!"*

○ Tasks that seem stupid – *"This is so lame."*

○ Poor perception of end product – *"Gosh. I can't picture this. What's it supposed to look like once I'm done?"*

○ Perceived injustice – *"It's not fair that I have to do this!"*

○ Utter dislike of the task – *"I HATE math!"*

○ Short-sightedness – *"The due date is still a long way off."*

Fears and Other Feelings

○ Fear of success – *"If I do too well, I'll always* have *to do well."*

○ Fear of failure – *"If I do poorly, then others will think less of me."*

○ Emotions like unhappiness or embarrassment – *"I'm feeling upset, so I'm not doing this!"*

○ Fear of being too profound – *"If I do it the way I really want, it'll be far too advanced."*

○ Mood – *"I don't feel like it."*

○ Feeling overwhelmed – *"A thousand other things need my attention right now."*

○ Anxiety – *"I'm so stressed out. My head's pounding. I think I'm gonna faint!"*

○ Dirtiness or offended senses – *"Dissecting frogs? I'll gag! They feel slimy, it's gross, and I can't stand the smell."*

○ Avoid punishment – *"I'll tell them* later *that I broke that vase."*

○ Fear of ridicule – *"What if I do this wrong and then everyone makes fun of me?"*

Outside Influences

○ Lack of information – *"I really don't know what's expected of me."*

○ Temptation – *"I'd much rather play with my puppy (toys, friends) than do that!"*

○ Technological interference – *"I have to check Facebook, download photos, send a few text messages, and add tunes to my playlist before I can do anything else."*

○ Fun factor – *"Homework and chores aren't as much fun as doing other stuff."*

○ Disorganization and poor planning – *"I have to get rid of the clutter and make some kind of a plan before I can begin."*

○ Expectations – *"My parents expect too much of me. I'll never satisfy them."*

○ Desire to conform – *"I'll wait for others to do it first."*

○ Weather – *"It's such a beautiful day! Tomorrow may rain, so I'm going to play outside while I can."*

○ Interfering familial factors – *"There's too much happening at home right now."*

Well-being

- ○ Poor health – *"I don't feel up to it today."*

- ○ Fatigue – *"I haven't been sleeping well. I'm too tired."*

- ○ Distractions – *"I can't concentrate. It's so noisy! I work better when it's quiet."*

- ○ Time out – *"I need a break."*

- ○ Physical discomfort – *"It's hot in here. And I'm hungry."*

- ○ Sensing danger – *"I could get injured or something bad could happen."*

- ○ Low energy level – *"I just don't have the energy."*

Attitude or Temperament

- ○ Save the excitement – *"I'll set this aside, and then I'll have something to look forward to!"*

- ○ Autonomy or need for control – *"I'll set my own rules and timelines."*

- ○ Lack of responsibility – *"If I put it off, maybe someone else will do the work instead."*

- ○ Blasé attitude – *"It'll get done—eventually..."*

- ○ Pestering factor – *"I'll do this once people stop nagging and just leave me alone."*

- ○ Over-confidence – *"I can take my time and still finish early."*

- ○ Pay off – *"What's in it for me if I do it now as opposed to later?"*

- ○ Manipulation – *"If I wait long enough, my parents will promise me something good when I finally agree to start and then finish the work on time."*

- ○ Settling – *"If I don't do the work, I'll still get a C in the course. I can live with that."*

- ○ Track record – *"Nobody really expects me to start on time, so why disappoint them?"*

- ○ Easy justification – *"Everyone procrastinates."*

Personal Sensibilities

○ Recognizing priorities – *"First things first. I have real issues to deal with. This can wait."*

○ Brainstorming – *"I need to work it out creatively with others before I can start."*

○ Knowing one's pace – *"My brain just isn't wired to work quickly. I need lots of time."*

○ Delegating – *"He'll do it better, faster, and with less hassle."*

○ Wanting time to reflect – *"I have to think about it more carefully first."*

○ Controversy – *"Everyone has different opinions about this stuff. I don't want to get involved yet."*

○ Stepping back – *"I'll wait. Things will settle down."*

○ Memory – *"The last time I did something like this it was horrible! I don't want to go through that again."*

○ Global concerns – *"Who cares about adding decimals? I'd rather know how they're going to contain that huge oil spill and save the endangered fish and animals."*

○ Little interest or relevance – *"What connection can this possibly have with my life?"*

○ Previous experiences reinforcing the behavior – *"I got away without doing the last assignment—hey, no problem."*

Lacking Requirements

○ Not having the right equipment or work space – *"I need a proper desk, more paper, a daily planner, and a new lamp."*

○ Wanting a coach – *"If only I had some coaching, then I'd be able to deal with it properly."*

○ Lack of clarity and uncertainty as to how to begin – *"Oh dear! Where do I start?"*

○ Poor modeling at home – *"My parents put things off all the time yet they manage okay."*

○ Weak technological skills – *"I'm not very good with computers."*

○ Assistance – *"I need help with this!"*

Once your child has given some thought to these and other possible reasons for procrastinating, you might explore with him the ones he checks off. For example, the first reason that appears on the list is *looming large*. If your child placed a checkmark there, then it becomes something to discuss. This is the view that whatever he has to tackle is *BIG*—too unwieldy, too difficult, too much to cover, too little time—so why bother? Consider together, what makes a particular task too big? Is it really an actual problem that would affect well-being? Or is it a perception, such that the task looks bigger than it actually is? And whose problem is it? The child's? (*"Can't do it!"*) The parent's? (*"Should do it!"*) The professional's? (*"Required to do it!"*) What are the facts and opinions? And what can a parent do to encourage the desired behavior? Of course, the goal is for your child to become self-regulating and to complete required tasks on his own, but he may need help at first until time management becomes an easier skill for him.

Here are sample strategies that might come out of such a discussion to help a child get going on a task:

Figure 1.2. Dealing with Looming Large

○ **Pin it down.** Clarify expectations and why the task matters.

○ **Start small.** Label doable chunks. An hour or so of purposeful physical activity or sports on a daily basis may be fine for some kids. Others may not be so inclined, or they may be pressed for time, so they procrastinate. Stretching, doing a few exercises, and then gradually increasing activities to help stay fit may be a more realistic ambition—from which to build, and take pleasure.

○ **Is the deadline flexible?** See if there is any leeway with respect to deadlines.

○ **Compare it to something familiar.** Think about similar tasks and how you managed the timeline for those.

○ **Find success stories.** Think about people who prevailed or stories about characters who "moved mountains"—or conversely, people who stalled needlessly because they "made mountains from molehills."

○ **Find help.** Ask for assistance or guidance. There's no shame in that. Chat about where to find additional information, how to respectfully approach someone who might be able to provide support, and how to politely request direction.

○ **Share the load.** Collaborate with others.

○ **Give yourself a pep talk.** "I can do this if I try!" Resolve to continue to think optimistically and confidently.

This process of acknowledging the reason for procrastination, identifying if it's truly a problem (e.g., a situation that could impede health, personal growth, academic achievement, or relationships), and talking about it together so as to figure out how to deal with it *now* can help a child learn to manage and overcome procrastination.[4]

If a youngster prefers to work through this checklist independently, encourage him to do so. Hopefully he won't procrastinate, but if he does, ask why and add it to the list!

Procrastination is a personal matter, and understanding what spurs or compromises a person's productivity is not always easy. It requires some reflection. And, by the way, the reasons for procrastination listed in Figure 1.1 can apply to adults, too, and provide a basis for thought, renewed focus, and action.

Procrastination: The Broader View

Procrastination does not always result in inefficiency, nor does it automatically reflect substandard behavior. Some industrialized countries place greater importance than others on punctuality where a sense of purpose is aligned with a timeline.[5] In North America, we have come to see timelines as important because efficiency and productivity are often emphasized at work places, including schools. Workload pressure may spill over into the home. Kids watch their parents cope with pressure and timelines, and begin to develop strategies for responsibilities they will inevitably face when they grow up. Overall, it makes good sense to accomplish tasks *at a personal pace* at which one can persevere, overcome obstacles and setbacks, and succeed in meeting goals. However, parents may have a hard time accepting this when it comes to their child's time management tendencies, especially if his pace and theirs don't match. Sometimes children take longer than anticipated to process instructions, a new skill, or a response to a request, and even longer to get started on it. Parents, particularly those who tend to do things quickly, may have to allocate more time for a child to complete a task.

Some parents strongly discourage procrastination, and their children are not allowed to deviate from expected standards.[6] These children adhere to strict guidelines with respect to homework and other obligations. Cultures differ in their rules and requirements and in the methods they use to enforce them. When children procrastinate, some parents take a very authoritarian approach, whereas others are permissive, and still others emphasize patient persistence.

Children can and often do procrastinate—indeed they learn the word *No!* very early on. Before long, they know how to use it—meaningfully, too. Studies show that procrastination increases with every year in school. Approximately 75% of college students identify themselves as procrastinators; half of college students say this is a consistent problem. In contrast, within the general population, only 25% of adults define themselves as procrastinators, and procrastination drops significantly after several years in the workplace.[7] Perhaps this can be attributed to the fact that working environments tend to operate on strict deadlines with clear natural consequences for procrastination, and those who can adhere to timely behaviors often succeed and stay in their jobs, while those who cannot may lose their jobs.

As you think about your child's procrastination, consider also how *you*, at times, have overcome the desire to procrastinate. Lisa Rivero, author of *A Parent's Guide to Gifted Teens* writes, "I chuckle at how often we parents complain about our children's procrastination and in the next breath rattle off all the items on our to-do list that are unfinished because we can't seem to motivate ourselves."[8] Strategies parents use to overcome their own motivational issues can become valuable lessons for children. You can share these stories with your children when you empathize with their own procrastination. Help them understand that this is something you have experienced and overcome. Point out that they can take control of their actions if they try and that you are there to offer ongoing support.

Informal surveys I have conducted over the course of several recent education conferences with hundreds of people have convinced me that individuals typically recognize procrastination tendencies in themselves. I ask attendees, most of whom are parents, "How many of you admit that you procrastinate on some tasks?" Time after time, everyone's hand goes up, generally accompanied by sheepish giggles and grins and a sense of relief as people look around the room to see all the others whose hands are raised.

Honestly, who hasn't procrastinated at some point in their life? Who hasn't sent belated birthday wishes or postponed responding to phone calls, letters, or e-mails? What about doing laundry, cleaning beneath the fridge, or checking that the smoke detectors are working properly? Ask your friends and family members and see if they have procrastinated. They may have even put off thinking about it or admitting it. [9]

Parents should understand that while a child's procrastination isn't something that should be praised, it does not always merit scolding or reproach. Sometimes people—young, old, and in-between—just need help getting past whatever is causing the procrastination in the first place, along with some good old-fashioned encouragement and support. Also think about how large a problem the procrastination is. It may not be quite as bad or big as one thinks. Is it a stone, rock, boulder, or mountain? Is there a simple way to eliminate, reduce, get around, or scramble over it?

Developing the ability to match a strategy and a time frame to the scope of a task can take time and perseverance. It may also require specific tactics, monitoring, and lots of patience. Procrastination is, in fact, an appropriate course of action in certain situations. More about those reasons, their authenticity, how they apply to children, and how to strive toward deleting delay is in the next chapter.

CHAPTER 2

Procrastination:
To Do or Not to Do?

"It's a job that's never started that takes the longest to finish."
~ J. R. R. Tolkien

Procrastination is something that most people do, but when is it reasonable to procrastinate? When is it a problem? Can we use our common sense about procrastination?

Of course, parents want their children to acquire common sense and use it liberally and wisely. We have all seen examples of what can happen when common sense is lacking. Suzanne didn't read the assigned novel and so she failed her term test. Jack couldn't be bothered to go back upstairs to get his sweater and his skates. He was cold on the way to school and then missed skating in a hockey trial and wasn't eligible to play in the big tournament. Noreen never got the materials she needed to sew her square for the school's Remembrance Day quilt. The memorial project was completed and displayed in the town hall—minus her piece. Liam put off writing his college applications and lost a chance for a scholarship. Perhaps these kids lacked common sense, but, more likely, they chose not to use it. They probably knew the consequences of their actions would not be favorable. Yet they did not use that foresight or take into account the possible nature or extent of those outcomes. Common sense involves using good judgment, and most children are not overly experienced at that.

We cannot measure common sense, but we know it when we see it. When outcomes are good, we often think common sense had something to do with it. When outcomes are bad, like missing tournaments or scholarship opportunities, we often bemoan a child's lack of common sense. More planning or time or effort could have saved the day.[10]

It's just common sense that to complete something you have to begin. Accomplishment is a process. Like walking along a pathway, the first step leads to the next, and the next, and so on. All manner of distractions may lie along the way, but until you take that first step you will never know the possibilities, pitfalls, or pleasures of the pathway.

If you are a procrastinator, that first step can be the hardest one of all. Sometimes a person will delay taking an initial step until an opportunity is gone, and suffers the consequences. On the other hand, even if he does get going, there may be reasons to pause or stop altogether while en route.

Sometimes we postpone something for "good reason." For example, a teenage girl decides to buy winter boots a bit later in the season since the December weather has been unusually warm. She thinks the boots she likes will go on sale before it snows. It seems like a sensible course of action. A boy trying to choose a song to showcase his voice takes extra time to listen to many different tunes and still cannot settle on a particular melody to perform at his school recital. He puts it off until he has a chance to talk about it with his friends. These examples represent thoughtful, common sense choices that involve putting things off.

About Procrastination: What Is It? Who Does It? When and Why?

Helping kids overcome detrimental procrastination is a challenge, harder even than overcoming your own. It is often more difficult to discover the root of their procrastination. Maybe it has to do with capability. Sometimes the endpoint is just too far away; the goal may seem unreachable or pointless. Maybe the child perceives obstacles ahead or thinks there is some sort of danger involved. Or maybe the timing is wrong; there are better things to do or more interesting places to go. Like common sense, procrastination is not easy to pin down. However, by looking carefully at the underlying tendencies, we can gain some understanding of why children—and adults—procrastinate, and what we can do about it.

The most common complaints about procrastination usually concern a child's schoolwork. Since parents do not often get to see what happens over the course of a school day, let's peek into a hypothetical classroom where a number of students have not completed their assignments.

It is almost the end of the school year for everyone in Miss Gilroy's calculus class.[11]

Oliver knows that he is behind schedule with his math work, but he thinks he can wait a day or two before it catches up with him. He seems preoccupied and moody. He has been like that at home, too.

Sharleen is an excellent student, but she is refusing to do the final math activity. She won't say why. She simply told her teacher that she will get to it next week instead—and then clammed up.

Katrina is absent. Again. She is avoiding math class altogether and has decided that the assignments no longer matter anyhow; it is nearly the end of the school year, and she decides she will study math come September.

Ben is not exactly sure what he has to do, and he doesn't want to investigate it now. He's doodling. He has resolved to wait till the moment is right to ask questions—whenever that may be. In the meantime, his abstract doodle pattern is becoming bigger and more intricate.

Each of these children is putting off the task until some other time, but the reasons for their procrastination are not the same.

Actually, Oliver has lots of other work due at the moment and he is prioritizing. He is an A student and usually gets all his assignments in on time, but right now he is swamped with juggling his workload and focused on sorting out what he has to do.

Sharleen, on the other hand, is really worried about problems at home. Her parents have been arguing over money matters, and she is feeling confused and distracted by all the heated discussions. She doesn't want to tell anyone about it, but she's upset. She can't concentrate on calculus.

Katrina already knows the math at this level (and more), and she is totally bored in class. She has repeatedly asked her teachers for more interesting and challenging activities, but it seems like no one ever listens. She has come to the conclusion that it doesn't make a difference what she does or doesn't do at this point in the school year.

Ben is uncomfortable about making mistakes. Calculus is not his best subject, and he has made several errors in his work over the past semester. He thinks that if he could just get some additional direction, then he would feel better about doing the assignment. He's embarrassed about asking for help, so he waits and hopes someone else will ask his questions for him.

For each of these children, tackling things at a later point in time seems like a pretty good idea. Yet if we were to use the word *procrastinator* to describe them, it would somehow convey a negative connotation. Why is that?

Somewhere along the line, the word procrastination evolved from "putting off until tomorrow" (from the Latin, *pro–crastinare*) to "dawdling" or "opting out." In some instances, words like "idle" or even "slothful" may come to mind. The emphasis has shifted from one of self-regulation, or sequencing activities a certain way for specific reasons, to one of self-sabotage or lack of ambition, energy, or responsibility.

There seems to be a moral dimension attached to procrastination; dragging one's feet is viewed as a behavior only to be criticized, even though a person may simply be waiting with good cause. Consider how parents and teachers may admonish a child for being lazy or slow to start something, when in fact he may be taking his time weighing options, planning, reflecting, or working on the task elsewhere with others.

It is important to try to understand why a person is procrastinating. Being too quick to label someone a procrastinator can impede his productivity, erode his self-confidence, make him feel less capable, and even devalue his accomplishments. It may make more sense to think of procrastination not as a way *out,* but rather a way *around* or *another way* altogether.

Let's go back to that classroom for a moment. Miss Gilroy, the math teacher, is very focused on getting through the course content before the end of term. She is assigning a lot of work, even though she understands that calculus can be very difficult for some students. However, she is frustrated because Oliver, Sharleen, Katrina, and Ben are all capable learners and, to her mind, they are not putting forth their best effort in her subject area. She sees their procrastination as willful disregard for her assignments, and she attributes their response to stubbornness, a poor attitude, laziness, or some other less than admirable cause. She recently placed calls to each of their parents, telling them that their children are not "working up to potential." To make matters worse, several other students have also neglected to hand in their work on time. Miss Gilroy is losing patience. However, truth be told, she herself has been known to take a prolonged time completing her marking.

It does not occur to Miss Gilroy that there are many different types of procrastinators—and many different reasons for deferring action. We have some idea as to why Oliver, Sharleen, Katrina, and Ben are procrastinating. Respectively, they are experiencing work overload, stress, lack of motivation, and apprehension about the subject matter.[12] Miss Gilroy may not be aware of what underlies her students' behavior, and so she is not sympathetic to them.

All of these children are bright and capable, and all feel they have a good reason for procrastinating. They are not being belligerent about it (those who are usually do not know how else to vent their frustration); they are just purposefully idling or otherwise occupied.[13] In many respects, they are doing their best to get by from one day to the next, carving out their own time frames for meeting demands. Supportive teaching and parenting will help them learn what they can manage and that they can succeed.

Procrastination Personas

Procrastination is no secret. Like caution, hesitation, and indecision, it's a slice of life. Stories abound about procrastinators. From one author to another, one culture to the next, fairy tale to nonfiction, we have all heard about individuals who have either benefitted or lost because someone deliberately chose to put off taking action of some sort. Perhaps most well known is the hare from Aesop's Fable "The Tortoise and the Hare." Think also of Scarlett O'Hara's famous line in Margaret Mitchell's *Gone with the Wind*: "Tomorrow I'll think of some way... After all, tomorrow is another day."[14] She waited, hoping for the best. Alternatively, consider this insightful perspective written by the young Anne Frank: "How wonderful it is that nobody need wait a single moment before starting to improve the world."[15] Anne's view was that by taking positive action as soon as possible the world would become a better, more humane place. In the famous folk tale "Stone Soup," people would have gone hungry were it not for the fact that an enterprising individual got started with nothing more than a pot of water and a stone, and then, one by one, others had the initiative (and good sense) to add something to the pot.[16] Before long, things were bubbling along.[17]

What type of person procrastinates? As you can see from examples of procrastinators across differing cultures and genres, there is no one typical character profile; there are, however, some familiar personas that may loosely match procrastinators you know.[18] On the following pages you'll see a collection of character sketches that may help identify what underlies your own procrastination tendencies and those of others. Before developing and trying strategies to resolve procrastination, it is valuable to consider the possible causes. Since there can be many reasons why a person procrastinates, the 24 procrastinator profile sketches listed are really just a sampling. They do not include everyone, but they should be more than enough to get you thinking. See if any of these profiles resonates for you. You will also see how the procrastinator might be feeling. For each portrayal, there are one or two specific strategies parents can use to help kids deal with the tendency to put things off.

With virtually all of the 24 procrastinator personas, there are some general approaches that may help reduce a problem of procrastination. Sometimes it is as simple as finding a way to minimize the problem. For example, a child who has difficulty making choices can be given fewer options to choose from. Narrow down his options to just a few books, less time for a task, or a shorter to-do list. Other times, coming to terms with procrastination is not quite as simple and could take more time and strategizing. For instance, choosing courses or writing a term paper (or a book like this!) can be labor intensive. Maybe there are worries to confront and address. Solutions will vary because people do.

Throughout this book, you will find many ideas to use, and there are strategies in checklists at the end of sections dealing with particular areas of focus. Each description in Figure 2.1 and its accompanying suggestions represent only a starting point for parents as they think about how to help their children overcome procrastination.

Figure 2.1. Procrastination Personas

The Perfectionist – The perfectionistic procrastinator is driven and has lofty expectations. She feels she has to do everything *just so*, which often makes the task at hand appear much more daunting than it truly may be. She spends more time and energy than necessary on things and may opt *not* to do a task, or avoid it for as long as possible, rather than risk imperfection.

"If I can't get 100% on that math assignment then I'd better not do it."

Suggestion: Build in interim check-points or chunk the workload into smaller more doable segments to promote a sense of accomplishment.

The Pressure Pot – Some procrastinators live on the edge and enjoy the frenzied appeal of doing something last minute—whether it is cramming for a test, scurrying to beat a deadline, or always being late to meet friends. This type of procrastination provides an adrenalin rush for the individual, literally and figuratively.

"I love the feeling I get when I have to scramble to get things done!"

Suggestion: Redirect the charge of energy to channel it earlier, or toward specific activities. Ask friends to provide early reminders of due dates or meeting times. (No one likes to be kept waiting.)

The Immediacy Reactor – These people live spontaneously and they tend to have difficulties with due dates and timelines. They would rather squeeze joy out of every minute, responding to whatever happens to be taking place around them presently, not whatever is due later.

"There's going to be a great party at Angelo's tonight. Homework can wait!"

Suggestion: Set ground rules to avoid getting off track. For example, on school nights (including Sundays), homework comes first. Parties, television, or video games may come later.

The Rebel – Sometimes people procrastinate as a way of rebelling or making a personal statement. Putting something off is an action-equivalent of declaring "Why should I do this when you say?" Behavior can range from simply standing firm, to resisting rules, to more oppositional action or outright refusal to comply.

"I'll do it when I want to. So there!"

Suggestion: Model and teach respect. Often rebellious behaviors are about the relationship with a parent or teacher. Focus on relationship issues or even withdraw from insisting on completion of the task and avoid a power struggle.

The Lazy Bones – Yes, some people *are* just lazy. Maybe there are medical, emotional, or other reasons that lead to their lethargy. Or they may lack initiative because it suits them at that particular time or in that particular situation.

"Yawn."

Suggestion: Is the child well-rested and in good health? Fatigue can play a big role in lack of motivation. Aside from getting more sleep, there are many ways to motivate kids. Help them plan "work times" for when they know they are most rested. You can start by having them keep a journal or calendar of times when their energy level is highest and co-create a schedule around those times.

The Ditherer – This procrastinator struggles to make decisions, and when confronted with one or more alternatives (should I tackle this or that?), may opt to do nothing while weighing the possibilities. The decision to deliberate and dither is a decision in its own right.

"I don't know what to do first. I'll wait—for a sign."

Suggestion: Ask them if they are more comfortable starting with something that is easy or more difficult, active or quiet. Fewer decisions make deciding easier.

The Exceeder – Some individuals focus so much on achievement or appeasing people that they take on way too much as a way to please others, or themselves. They go over the top, and then time management can become problematic. It may be hard for them to say *no*, and they feel stressed that, as a result, some things have to be put on the back burner for another day.

"I can't do it all! Help!"

Suggestion: Show kids how to decline gracefully when asked to juggle too many responsibilities, without feeling guilty about it. They can take note of how others kindly and effectively decline, and they can learn to prioritize opportunities or tasks.

The Muddler – Not everyone finds it easy to make sense of everything that requires attention. Sometimes instructions or expectations are not clear enough or a task appears too difficult, and then a person gets muddled. There is less likelihood that tasks will get started, let alone completed where there's confusion, complexity, or chaos.

"Huh?"

Suggestion: Clarification often makes a task less complicated. Parents can encourage their children to speak up when in need of assistance, whether it's something they are asked to do at home (like helping to set up for a family celebration,) or something that is school related (like creating a diorama to illustrate a study topic).

The Casual Cavalier – This person is a visionary with lots of plans and aspirations. However, he has so many hopes and dreams that they are distracting. Such a multitude of ideas and a million things to do! Some just have to be put on hold.

"I'm going to read about giraffes, and build a kite, and make a model of that volcano that erupted in Iceland, and find out why some onions in our fridge have roots and others don't, and invent a new flavor of ice cream, and..."

Suggestion: What is most important and why? Teach children to prioritize, but be sure to include some fun and creative activities as well. Help kids figure out what needs doing first so they can accomplish those things expediently, with the idea that they can still have plenty of time to design that kite, peel those onions, and poke through the kitchen cupboards for intriguing ice cream flavor combinations!

The Dangler – Skipping around from one task to another inevitably leaves some undone, or dangling. These tasks may not regain attention and if left hanging, they may never get done.

"Maybe I'll get back to this later. And that, and those other things too..."

Suggestion: Explain the many benefits of sticking to one thing at a time—it can prevent distractions, shoddiness, and overload. Better still, help children discover the benefits for themselves. For example, if they want to make cookies, and do Sudoku puzzles, and dance to Bruno Mars, they may need help focusing on one activity at a time. So maybe just let the cookies get burnt, and they'll get the idea.

The Fretter – The Fretter procrastinates because he does not like to take risks. *What if...?* is a constant refrain going through his mind as he approaches one task or another, so he puts it all off until it seems less daunting.

"What if I get it all wrong, or people laugh at me, or the end results turns out looking disgustingly awful?"

Suggestion: Look at and discuss the broader picture. Think, so what? How big a deal is that? Consider playing the "worst case scenario" game. For example, will it matter in five years? In 10 years? What is the evidence to support each scenario?

The Smooth Operator – Highly capable individuals may feel that they can and will achieve, and therefore they do not need to push themselves to do so quickly. They have learned to be efficient and resourceful, and their record for accomplishment speaks for itself. They count on their proficiency and rest assured that, ultimately, they will get the task done.

"No problem. I don't need that much time."

Suggestion: Show children how completing a task quickly can be used to even greater advantage if there is time left at the end to extend ideas further. Moreover, more time means more opportunity to think, review, practice, or do whatever it takes to improve the quality of the product, whether it is a homework assignment, an exercise routine, or something else altogether.

The Struggler – In some cases, people are unable to figure out or fulfill the demands of a task because they just do not possess the capability or requisite skills to do so. For example, some children may be placed in an advanced-level class when they are not advanced in that particular subject, or others may find assigned work too hard. Inability can affect motivation to begin an activity, or to carry on.

"I just can't do this!"

Suggestion: Provide scaffolding—that is, assistance and guidance as necessary—and also look at alternative ways to tackle a particular task. Also, teach self-advocacy so kids learn how to ask for help when they feel they need it.

The Otherwise Occupied – Life can be hectic and eventful. The term "busy body" has taken on new meaning, with an emphasis on *busy*. Days and nights may be loaded with demands and activities. Plus, there is music to listen to, social media to manage, workouts to do, and family and friends to see.

"So much to do, so little time!"

Suggestion: Help children create, use, and adhere to a daily agenda so as to better organize their lives. Purchase a small ready-made calendar that is appealing and well designed, and encourage them to keep it handy. Block in work time first—and refer to the calendar!

The Relaxer – When days are really full, there are fewer oportunities to relax. Down-time, play, rest, and peaceful moments can be very important. Sometimes they can take precedence over doing other kinds of activities.

"I need a chance to unwind first."

Suggestion: Help children schedule breathers and time for leisure. And then encourage them to actually take that time.

The Doubter – Procrastination can result from not having enough confidence about one's abilities. Uncertainty and insecurity compromise a person's self-assurance and initiative, and this kind of doubt or timidity can affect productivity.

"I'm not sure... I dunno... I've never been good at math."

Suggestion: Review children's past successes with them, including the steps they took in order to be successful.

The Sleeper – Making snap judgments or acting too quickly can prove to be detrimental. "Sleeping on it" is an approach some people use to stall decision-making or action—for better or worse. Sometimes this tactic becomes a habit, lasts longer than overnight, and may be perceived by others as laziness.

"Whoa! Not so fast!"

Suggestion: Teach children how to recognize what requires immediate attention and what they can put to rest for the time being. For example, learning to be safe online is important, even though it may require many steps and attention to detail. These can be emphasized—along with a plan for time-outs.

The Groaner – Not everyone is blessed with a cheery disposition. Some people seem to be crabby by nature; alternatively, they may have very legitimate reasons for being cranky. Procrastination may be a way of acting out these feelings.

"Yuck."

Suggestion: Empathize with children, and discuss sensible ways to vent. When a child is irritable and refuses to comply—perhaps it has been an extremely busy day, or he is upset for some other reason—

give him ample opportunity to talk about what he is feeling or what is bothering him. It is okay for him to cry, clench his fists, and take a breather. Practical strategies for helping kids develop emotional intelligence are widely available.[19]

The Careless Custodian – This down-ward spiraler just does not realize the importance of taking care of herself when it comes to things like resting, eating properly, exercising, etc., and then because of her waywardness, she's not up to task.

"What's the problem?"

Suggestion: Don't nag, but do discuss the importance of maintaining a healthy lifestyle. Mention some of the obvious benefits, like feeling stronger, more alert, and receptive, and ask your child to come up with her own reasons. That can generate some thought and account-ability.

The Boaster – The Boaster procrastinates because he likes attention and revels in the satisfaction of knowing that he can accomplish something at the last minute. Perhaps he will pull off a major assign-ment in a matter of days or hours, or finish a difficult task in record time even though it's close to the deadline—and then he can let others know about his feat.

"Hey! Look what I pulled off!"

Suggestion: Point out other means of getting attention. Kids who can accomplish things at the 11th hour can be encouraged to use the lead-up time productively by doing something creative or by helping others who may be struggling with a similar task. This draws a better response than boasting.

The Analyst – Critical thinking is important in *all* aspects of life but taking it too far can be counterproductive and consume too much time and energy.

"There's so much to think about!"

Suggestion: Teach children who see too many possibilities to find the best ones for *this* task. Sometimes deciding on specific criteria helps.

The Pickup Artist – The pickup artist may start off focused and with good intentions but along the way she finds (or picks up) other things she wants to attend to. So one thing gets shelved or postponed while another takes precedence, and then another...

"I never noticed that before. I better check it out."

Suggestion: Tap the idea "not now, maybe later" so it becomes a useful strategy! Help kids work out a recording system so when they are tempted to stray off track, they mark it down so that it's not really sidelined—just "starred" or put "on notice" till later. Knowing they will be able to pay attention to the matter when there is more time to devote to it means they can consciously refocus on the task at hand.

The Forget-Me-Not – Disorganized procrastinators, or even those who seem to be organized and put things on to-do lists, can sometimes forget to follow through. When lists become too long, it is hard to remember what's on them—or even where they are! Taking action belatedly or missing timelines may be unhealthy, awkward, or embarrassing.

"I meant to do it, but I forgot."

Suggestion: Record on a calendar whatever is being set aside—right then and there—and clearly indicate when it has to be completed. Visible reminders will help jog the memory so things can get done.

The Artful Dodger[20] – Some procrastinators enjoy a ruse or a little harmless deception. They are rascally, maybe mischievous. For them, procrastination is a ploy. They get a charge out of devising excuses for not doing things—and seeing what they can get away with.

"Heh, heh, heh..."

Suggestion: Discuss accomplishment—it is a process, not a game— and offer some real life examples about why trickery and deceptive schemes really do not pay.

Procrastination can occur anytime, anywhere, to anyone, and behavior can be specific to certain situations. Someone who exhibits one style of procrastination in one subject area or aspect of life may show a different procrastination style, or none at all, in another.

Miss Gilroy, the math teacher, is an *Exceeder* at school and has assigned a lot of homework to the students, giving herself far too much grading as a result. Instead of encouraging students to self-evaluate some of their work over the course of the term, she has taken it upon herself to evaluate every single assignment, and she has let it pile up. However, when it comes to tidying her cluttered desk at home (something that she never seems to get to) she is more of a *Rebel* and doesn't really care if others think that her disarray is reflective of a disorganized mind. She instinctively knows that is not so. When she thinks about having to contact the parents of students who are procrastinating, she is quite a *Fretter*. She wants to keep them informed, but at the same time she doesn't want to raise alarms because it might reflect on her classroom management skills. She has waited till the end of the semester to make the calls, and it is almost too late for parents to help their children improve in that class.

On the other hand, Miss Gilroy never, ever procrastinates when it comes to reading the latest math journals. She really likes discovering the newest technological trends for teaching calculus and considers this an important part of teacher preparation.

Ways of thinking underlie how people act, or choose not to. And there are many reasons for thinking that procrastination is at times the best course of action. Those reasons, their authenticity, and how they apply to children are all keys in our efforts toward overcoming or managing procrastination.

To better understand practical approaches that help children beat procrastination, let's look at connections between procrastination and fundamental aspects of learning, because learning is integral to personal growth and accomplishment in all areas of life.

Chapter 3

Some Ties that Bind: Success, Failure, Stress, and Self-Regulation

"Things may come to those who wait, but only the things left by those who hustle."

~ Abraham Lincoln

A child's desire to learn is closely connected to his success. But to what do children attribute their success and their failure? Procrastination, after all, is linked to a child's ideas about achievement. For example, a youngster who has difficulty tying his shoelaces decides it is not worth the hassle and leaves them undone, or puts on a different pair of shoes instead. He defers learning to tie the laces. A student who does well in science but poorly in French class may spend an inordinate amount of time on lab experiments, but avoid doing her language work until the last possible moment. She procrastinates when it comes to any assignments in French class. A child who falls off a bike may wait a long time before summoning up the courage to try once more. He puts off learning the skill. Earlier I pointed out that there can be many reasons for procrastination, and that it is not always a bad thing. However, we want our children to be thoughtful about it. Whether their procrastination is detrimental is often determined by their self-talk and what they believe about themselves.[21]

This chapter is about how children view their successes and failures, how they handle stress, and how or if they are able to self-regulate.

Success

What factors make up the foundation of a person's success? Maybe it's skill, luck, assistance, opportunity, collaboration, strength, commitment, or influences at home, school, and in the community. These are all important, but the perception of success is also significant, as are hard work and perseverance.

Psychologist Carol Dweck, who is internationally respected for her work on mindsets, has conducted research on and documented the importance of effort.[22] The way people approach challenges and setbacks, as well as how much they are willing to engage in a task, strongly influences their success. This holds true for children and for adults; for people at school, in sports, at the work place, and even in relationships.

Dweck emphasizes the importance of cultivating a *growth mindset*—that is, the belief that you can develop your abilities over time if you have opportunities to learn and appropriate guidance and instruction. This *growth mindset* is quite different from a *fixed mindset*—that is, the belief that your abilities are predetermined and that there is not much you can do to improve or develop them. People with a fixed mindset are likely to give up on a challenging task rather quickly, and to procrastinate and postpone attempting what seems daunting to them. Regardless of ability level, a person's mindset is important. However, Dweck makes particular note of the concept of mindset in relation to bright children and adults. She writes, "To the extent that young people believe they simply have a gift that makes them intelligent or talented, they may not put in the work necessary to sustain that talent. Moreover, the gifted label that many students still receive, and that their parents relish, may turn some children into students who are overly cautious and challenge-avoidant lest they make mistakes, and no longer merit the label."[23]

An individual, no matter how smart or capable, cannot just expect to sit down at a piano and play a concerto, or apply complex mathematical theories, or consistently hit the bull's eye with a bow and arrow without putting forth the time and effort required to develop the necessary prerequisite skills in that particular area. Development of a particular skill set takes many hours of practice.

If parents and teachers want to nurture a child's willingness to take on tasks and to persist even when a task is hard, they should praise the child's growth-oriented *processes*—that is, their efforts—highlighting what they are able to accomplish through struggle, practice, study, and persistence (as opposed to, for example, speed or just glossing over things). For example, telling a child that she has done "a good job" on her clay sculpture is vague. Instead, you might say you appreciate how she has given careful consideration to the lines and texture of the piece, and worked hard on the shape. This gives her aspects to focus and build upon, and indicates *why* you think she has done a good job. This kind of specific praise emphasizes that productivity and high-level achievement come about as a result of work, perseverance, and thoughtfulness over time.

Some people equate procrastination with underachievement, but they are not the same. Procrastination does not necessarily kill achievement or success, but it can certainly thwart it. Individuals who put things off may lack the *impetus* to start or complete a task, but may get down to business and be successful in their own good time. Procrastination can lead to underachievement, or vice versa, and in some cases it becomes a spiraling scenario as one spurs the other. Stopping the cycle can be frustrating; parents may have to intervene and get to the root of the issue.

Children may underachieve or procrastinate for many of the reasons mentioned earlier, including a fear of being successful. Strange though it may seem, success can be daunting. It often leads to more success, which can become overwhelmingly intense as the bar is raised higher and higher. Success can trigger additional demands and expectations. This can become intimidating and even scary. Jocelyn, a top-notch seventh-grade student, fretted about being successful: "What if I get too tired trying to do everything everyone else wants? What if my friends become jealous of my success, or think I'm stuck up or showing off? What if other kids tease or bully me? What if success is not as great as people say it is?" Of course, it is not the continual success that is daunting; it is a person's perception of it and whether they have a growth mindset or a fixed mindset.

Fear of success can easily lead to uncertainty and procrastination. Sometimes it is just easier to stay within one's comfort level and to avoid striving for success or excellence, which pushes into realms that are potentially frightening, unknown, upsetting, or exhausting.

Again, it is not potential failure, but rather how a person thinks about success that can lead to the fear of it.

What can parents do to help children develop a mindset where they appreciate success rather than avoid or reject it? Figure 3.1 lists some practical ideas to help kids overcome procrastination tendencies that relate to fear of success.

Figure 3.1. Dealing with Fear of Success

○ **Talk with (not *to*) children about success.** Discuss why it is gratifying, motivating, and fun. Keep initial goals modest and celebrate small achievements. When children find joy in success, help them express their thoughts and feelings so they can better appreciate the pleasure, excitement, gratification, or pride.

○ **Reinforce children's initiative.** Praise their efforts to overcome procrastination tendencies, e.g., "I'm so pleased that you filled out the entry form for the Improv Festival! I know you've been thinking about it for a long time."

○ **Demonstrate effort, motivation, and pride in accomplishment.** Discuss why these matter. They help to build strengths and contribute to a sense of satisfaction.

○ **Encourage kids to reflect upon their past successes.** How did they feel? Excited? Fulfilled? Happy? Proud? Would they do anything differently? If so, what? And how might that be applied to their next challenge?

○ **Teach kids about a growth mindset.** Kids of any age can learn about mindsets. Communicate the idea in ways that are understandable. Figure out the mindset of the child —that is, what she is saying to herself about a particular task or activity.

○ **Share personal successes.** Parents can talk about the steps they took, and how they managed along the way.

Failure

A person afraid to fail or unable to cope with his mistakes may use procrastination as an escape from the situation, or just to stay on an even keel. Earlier we met Ben, a student who puts off doing his calculus homework because of mistakes in the past. He fears that he will fail the class, so he procrastinates to avoid facing the outcome. This is an example of "failure with honor" because he can tell himself that there is still the chance that he might have succeeded if only he had gotten through the task he was assigned.[24]

Some people dwell on negatives; they think they will do poorly on a given activity or predict things will turn out badly. They think of themselves as "losers" and blame themselves for lacking competence to manage a task. They may believe their failings and mistakes reflect lack of ability. Putting the matter off provides a way to save face. They believe it is better to be thought of as unhurried or late than to fail outright. Remember the personas from the previous chapter? The Fretter, the Muddler, or the Doubter may have thoughts like this.

Dweck's psychology research is also about understanding failure. She writes that "People in a growth mindset don't just seek challenge, they thrive on it," and she recognizes that those who lack this mindset typically have to strive to get past perceived limitations.[25] A person with a fixed mindset feels judged and evaluated all the time, and if he performs poorly during a task, he concludes that he is no good at it. People operating in this mindset do not want to jeopardize the status quo or open themselves up to possible criticism. They feel they have something to lose if they fail. If they don't try, they don't have to feel badly about their capabilities. By procrastinating, they avoid that possibility.

Twelve-year-old Genevieve had been taking synchronized swimming lessons for years. She and her teammates had won several city-wide awards. Now, they would be competing at an advanced level, against older, more experienced kids. Genevieve knew she was expected to put in many more hours of independent practice in order to build the skills she would need as an integral part of her team. Yet day after day, she put off going to the swimming pool. She knew what she *could* do—that is, what skills she had mastered—but she did not know what might happen if she tried to extend herself. This is an example of learned helplessness, a reluctance to try new skills that appear difficult or to accept a challenge that might show an inability to perform well. Learned helplessness is characterized by avoidance and a willingness to tackle only what is perceived as being "safe" or readily doable.[26]

In situations like this, emphasize a growth mindset—one that enables children to believe in themselves, to see possible opportunities rather than possible setbacks, and to harness their capabilities more productively. Provide them with a safe, dependable environment, and be an active listener. Children must feel that they are understood and will not be criticized if they try something and fail. Answer their questions honestly, while being mindful of their age and maturity, and they will come to trust your advice.[27] Explain how people benefit from mistakes. Show what a growth mindset looks like in action, including talking about your own frustration, persistence, and resilience. Sometimes adults are so hard on themselves that they forget that *everyone* started out by toddling, and that conquering challenging situations leads to feeling really good in the long run.

Think back to a time when you overcame a difficult set of circumstances or met a challenge head on. Remember those first few times behind the wheel as you learned to drive? What did you do to build self-confidence? Or perhaps you went skiing down a black diamond run? Remember looking down those steep, twisty slopes? How did you manage it? I recently rode a camel for the first time. I was terrified. At first I refused. This beast looked huge! I did not want to climb on its bristly uneven back and traipse across the sand, but my friends encouraged me to try and patiently waited for me to summon up the courage. It lumbered along unsteadily, and I was barely able to hold on. I thought I was going to fall off, but I prevailed! I felt a sense of accomplishment, and it was fun. (Sort of.)

Fear of failure can cause procrastination—as in, "I can't do this." But it can also end procrastination—as in, "I don't want to be labeled a failure." For example, Alexa was doing really well in art class. It was by far her favorite subject, and she had proven herself to be quite talented. All the same, she procrastinated, and had not even started on her big midterm project. She liked abstract painting, but this assignment was to draw a still life. She had already missed the due date, even though it had been extended for her—twice—when her mother received a phone call from the teacher: "Alexa is going to fail this course because she never handed in her art project." Her mother had no idea! The teacher continued, "I'll give her until tomorrow. She can do it! Last chance." Alexa's parents told her about the conversation and expressed their faith in her abilities. Alexa suddenly got very busy. She set up a bowl of fruit on the kitchen table, took out her charcoal sticks, and began to draw. The teacher's words were the trigger, and the fear of failing the course was both strong and motivating. She didn't want to fail, especially in art!

Encouraging words, from teachers, parents, friends and others, coupled with an unexpected or firm push can motivate someone to overcome procrastination. Figure 3.2 lists some additional ideas for parents whose children exhibit a fear of failure and who may procrastinate as a result.

Figure 3.2. Overcoming Fear of Failure

○ **Talk about the upside of perseverance.** Think of a time when the child kept at a task until it was completed or when a new skill was mastered after much effort. What helped the child be successful then?

○ **Help children learn to plan ahead.** List the steps involved in what they are going to do. Teach them how to plan backwards from the end of the project to where they are now to gauge the time each step will need. Try to anticipate obstacles to be better able to deal with them.

○ **There can be safety in numbers.** Sometimes being part of a group reduces the pressure. If there are stumbling points along the way, experiencing them together may take the edge off.

○ **Find a pattern or reoccurrence of difficulty that leads to procrastination.** Try charting it in order to work out how to tackle it. For example, a child avoids practicing the piano because she thinks she will never get past doing boring scales and playing the wrong notes. Plus, she wants to play a *real* song—something popular. Parents can help her understand how the scales can be melodic and build into familiar tunes. They can try to figure out the notes to a favorite song together or give her an opportunity to compose a song of her own. By charting chunks of time, she can go back and forth between creative activities and the more regimented and demanding practice that is required.

○ **Understand what failure is and is not.** Reassure children by explaining that when someone is not able to do something particularly well it doesn't mean he has failed. Do they have a favorite celebrity or someone whose accomplishments they follow? Have them check out the back story of these stars— even superstars don't excel all the time! We *all* have areas of strength and weakness. We all start as novices.

○ **Acknowledge the child's feelings.** Recognize that at times these may be intense. It may be hard for him to think or to express himself clearly. Offer a shoulder to lean on and a willingness to listen to any concerns. Be available to comfort him.

○ **Talk about how reason can help get past feelings like fear, sadness, or dismay**. Parents can acknowledge that the child is sad about not doing well on the history test, for example. When she is ready, they can generate some ideas together so she can improve her study skills and understandings of key historical events for next time.

○ **Teach kids about the process of trial and error, and how it relates to progress.** The kitchen is a handy spot for trial and error experiments. Constructing building-block towers can work, too. Stay alert for times when trial and error learning situations occur spontaneously.

○ **Reinforce effort.** Focus on the process not on the product. For instance, if a child worked on a poem or a script, parents can point out what she did well and how she developed the flow of creative ideas and worked hard to write realistic dialogue. Showing appreciation for effort helps kids capitalize on their strengths.

○ **Offer assistance if or as necessary.** This might be when they begin a task (when they may first procrastinate), as they work toward interim goals (when they may slow down), and as they approach the end goal (when they may need an extra boost).

Stress

Stress has many triggers. Remember Sharleen, the competent math student coping with a stressful situation at home? She has difficulty focusing on her schoolwork, and now she is procrastinating. Her parents have been arguing about finances, and Sharleen has been thinking about how she can help by looking into getting a part-time job. In the meantime, she is letting her schoolwork slide.

This can be a time when a family might work together to help redirect focus and reassure one another. Sharleen's parents may not be seeing eye-to-eye with one another on money matters, but it is important for them to pay attention to her, to recognize her feelings and concerns, and to think about the impact on her schoolwork. What is Sharleen telling herself about the situation and its implications? What is accurate, and what is not? Her parents could plan for regular and purposeful "family meeting" times, while assuring her that they are ready to talk with her whenever she wants. They could set aside time to talk about things—listening to her concerns, answering questions, validating views, and assuring her that there's transparency, mutual respect and honesty within the family circle. Sharleen could write down her thoughts or find ways to relax, perhaps through music, art, play, exercise, or sports. She might even benefit from talking with someone else—a professional counselor or a trusted friend or family member. This could go a long way toward allaying Sharleen's concerns and helping her get back on track with schoolwork and productivity.

However, parents must be mindful of when to take action. There is no one right time for every problem, and parents will have to decide whether something is an emergency or less urgent. They may have to accept that "the middle of a hurricane is not the time to teach navigational skills" and the best thing they can do for the moment is to help the child stay calm.[28]

Recognize, too, that procrastination can be a symptom of several behavioral and emotional disorders, including depression, anxiety disorders, substance abuse, phobias, eating disorders, schizophrenia, and obsessive compulsive disorder. These conditions are serious, and when they arise, seek the advice of a trained professional. A family's pediatrician can provide recommendations and counsel for finding the appropriate medical or psychological services.

Of course, not all circumstances are dire, and procrastination can simply be a way for a child to protect herself from doing something that she believes threatens her sense of well-being. Procrastination frees up time to think things through. It can be a self-help mechanism that, for some people, provides a measure of control. Making a decision, even a decision to do nothing, may help them to feel calmer, especially if things around them seem to be spinning out of control. For Sharleen, the loss of control came from discord in the family. Avoidance is one means children may choose to cope with adversity.

Avoidance responses can be self-reinforcing, blocking out perceived hardship or danger, and thereby making the road ahead appear less troublesome. However, avoidance behavior or putting things off, "out of sight out of mind," can be a difficult habit to break. In some cases this provides a means to distance or detach oneself from a potential threat and to make harshness less harsh. In other words, procrastination becomes a plausible way to quiet the disquiet.

In some ways, procrastination is like a phobia. For example, Janelle is terrified of needles. Even though she has not been feeling well, she tells her parents she is fine because she fears that if she goes to the doctor she will have to get a needle. This behavior is dangerous because Janelle runs the risk of compromising her health.

Sam is afraid of public speaking. He has to do a presentation in the school auditorium in a couple of weeks and he is stressed about it. He knows the material, and he is okay talking before a small group, but the very thought of a full auditorium is more than he can bear. He has been thinking about how to postpone or avoid the presentation altogether. He is already pretty sure that he is going to have some aches and pains that day and may not be able to attend school.

Even the most intelligent individuals can experience phobias. An advanced student or a mature and highly competent adult may realize that their particular fear is, to some extent, unfounded, but it exists nonetheless.[29] They keep telling themselves that they will address the fear one day, but since it is not particularly pressing or debilitating, they procrastinate. Although, they are not proud of this, they may rationalize by saying that everyone has some kind of fear they choose not to meet head on—perhaps they are afraid of thunder or crowds or heights—and they plan to face their fear, one day.

What happens when people choose to avoid a difficult or frightening situation? What is likely to occur if they procrastinate? It reinforces their tendency to put things off, or, as in the case of Janelle who is afraid of needles, it can endanger their health. Phobic triggers, such as elevators, snakes, clowns, loud noises, or darkness cannot always be avoided. People with strong fears or phobias need to learn to manage their fears, once they feel ready to do so and possibly with the help of a psychologist trained in this area.[30] For some, this may be a difficult, and even lifelong, challenge.

Phobias and procrastination both have to do with feelings, personal experiences, and self-talk concerns leading to avoidance behavior. However, phobias and procrastination are both manageable.

A considerable amount of clinical literature focuses on how to address phobias and, in particular, children's phobias. A child's pediatrician should be able to suggest appropriate literature for helping kids overcome strong fears that could cause stress and that also factor into procrastination tendencies.[31]

Here are a few suggestions that work to address fears.

Relaxation and breathing exercises help lessen muscle tension, reduce anxiety, and instill a sense of calm. Rhythmic breathing— breathe in and count to eight, then breathe out and count to eight again—can have emotional and physical benefits. Some children would rather use imagery than breathing techniques, for example closing their eyes and picturing something pleasurable (such as a memory or a feeling). Other children find that listening to music can provide a measure of tranquility.[32] Breathing apps and other tech-based relaxation options are available for those who want to investigate them online.[33]

Help children recognize and think about possible outcomes; have them consider consequences and anticipate what will likely happen if they do not confront something or do not see it through.

Encourage them to practice managing their self-talk, that is, thinking intently about *why* they are afraid, what might happen, and whether any perceived danger can be mitigated somehow. This is discussed in more detail in Chapter 7. Engage children in role-playing situations where they can practice overcoming their fear. For example, if they are afraid to take gymnastics, perhaps they can go and watch, talk to other kids participating, and find out what they enjoy. If they are scared of swimming in deep water, they can work on the strokes on land (practicing various kicking movements with their legs or sculling motions with their arms) without putting all the components together or even going into the water until they are ready. Expose them gently and slowly to a fear, imagining it, and at the same time providing an unpressured and supportive milieu in which to develop a protective means of coping with it as a way of systematic desensitization.[34]

A parent's role is not easy, especially around the issue of stress. Being tuned in, patient, and resourceful will help set the stage for tackling these challenges.

Unfortunately, the consequences of avoidance and procrastination may include generating more stress as an avoidance cycle develops. Poor marks, criticism, blame, and self-condemnation can lead to self-criticism, a negative mindset, and a downward spiral. Other concerns may include a lack of confidence, disorganization, and feelings such as sadness and guilt. However, a procrastinator's distress can be eased through discussing matters. And if a person has a debilitating condition that keeps him from facing challenges or meeting responsibilities that, too, will affect the situation. For example, Miss Gilroy, the calculus teacher, may be more accepting of a child's seemingly poor task commitment and more accommodating of his needs if she knows that health-related concerns are keeping him from getting started on his work. Sometimes a student will hide behind a diagnosis and use it as a way to excuse his tardy or inappropriate behavior, and that needs to be addressed as well. Some kids use a variety of body aches and pains to avoid tasks or procrastinate, and it can be challenging for parents to not accidentally reinforce this avoidance behavior.

How can parents help kids overcome procrastination due to stress? And how can they lessen stress that occurs because of procrastination? Figure 3.3 lists some strategies:

Figure 3.3. Managing Stress

○ **Encourage open dialogue**. What is *really* bothering the child? Too much work? Too difficult? Too boring? Listen carefully, then discuss. Talk about stress—how a little can be energizing, how too much can be debilitating, and how everyone has times when things pile up. Parents can help children believe in themselves and their ability to cope with demands and situations by talking about and reinforcing positive actions and, in particular, the efforts they put forth.

○ **Use active listening.** Active listening describes a process in which the listener reflects or echoes the speaker, by rephrasing what has been said. It confirms a message and communicates understanding. Often used in counseling and training sessions, active listening can be useful for parents because it strengthens communication and enables kids to see adults making an effort to pay attention to their words *and* to the meaning behind them.

○ **Be alert to the particular times the child exhibits stress.** When does it occur? When there are pending due dates? Not enough sleep? Problems with friends? Try to identify and work together to eliminate specific triggers.

○ **Rely on routines**. Routines can be calming. Doing what comes normally provides a way for kids to feel organized and in control. It then also leaves time for them to get around to doing other things.

○ **Encourage downtime.** Help kids schedule time for breaks, play, and relaxation.[35]

○ **Keep in mind the acronym HALT—Hungry, Angry, Lonely, and Tired.**[36] All of these conditions magnify stress and need to be managed first. Children who know the acronym can recognize their needs and address them.

○ **Solicit help.** Consult with professionals if stress is becoming debilitating—the child's pediatrician, a school counselor, or other clinical practitioners should be able to offer useful advice or provide direction to someone well suited for the particular situation.

Self-Regulation

Self-regulation skills are essential for acting in timely and systematic ways.[37] Some procrastinators may never have learned the practical skills required to work efficiently or, at the very least, with an eye for timeliness. These skills include using self-talk and charting in order to track what needs to be done—such as clarifying instructions and expectations, organizing materials, scheduling periodic rest times, breaking tasks down into steps, and devising reasonable time frames for each one. Each is a separate skill set, although they work in combination, and they can be learned at home as well as at school.

Oliver, the A-level student who prioritizes his many assignments, has put together a timeline for his schoolwork. He makes regular entries in his calendar noting when he is going to tackle and complete his various assignments. He has decided to put his math work on the back burner for the time being. Miss Gilroy may think he is procrastinating, but Oliver sees his actions as strategic. Indeed, he is self-regulating.

Of course, some people could not care less when they get things done because timeliness is irrelevant to them. It is simply not part of their character to be concerned about timelines. They march to their own beat, at whatever speed suits them. If no one seems any worse for it, nothing changes. When this happens, parents may have to step back and allow their children to face the consequences of their actions (or lack thereof). That can be a turning point.

Some children have learning issues such as Attention Deficit Disorder (ADD), and experience difficulties with organization, impulse control, and task completion. There are many strategies that can be used to help them meet the challenges they confront.[38] Others may feel ill equipped because they were never taught how to do things as effectively as they would like. This can affect motivation and productivity.

Miss Gilroy's students could benefit, too, from some anticipatory praise.[39] She could preemptively provide that extra bit of incentive to push them forward with a little positive reinforcement or some amiable suggestions for how best to tackle a project well before its due date. Several days before the project is due, she might say, for example, "Oliver, I noticed you're scheduling your assignments, and I think it's great that you're working on planning and getting organized." Oliver may not yet be as adept at prioritizing and juggling assignments as he thinks he is, or as he'd like to be, but the positive reminder and praise is likely to help him focus. Everyone can benefit from some simple pointers on how to organize workloads.

Self-regulation involves being proactive about looking after one's own affairs, including behavior. It requires resolve and doggedness, especially when there are circumstances or distractions that tempt one to be less than productive. A little assistance from adults may be called for. Parents and teachers can help by modeling good organizational skills, and by recognizing that maturity increases (generally) with age, and that young children do not yet have sophisticated skill sets. Skill building takes time, instruction, and practice.

Ensure that children are familiar with and comfortable in their environment. Kids need a sensible framework by which to operate, e.g., this is what is expected; this is what is fair; this is how we do things and why. There is a lot to be said for organized stability.

Children's abilities to be and to stay organized can be compromised if they feel upset, frightened, or have other feelings that interfere with their day-to-day functioning. They can be taught to recognize their emotions—anger, fear, confusion, frustration, etc.—especially the ones that trigger avoidance, like fear. Other feelings, like dismay, embarrassment, bewilderment, guilt, and indignation can also be frontrunners leading to procrastination. Body language, tone of voice, and facial expressions can convey those emotions to adults who are on the lookout for such tells. There are programs and resources available to help children identify and cope with their emotions, and learn how to moderate and control those that get out of hand.[40]

Here are some more suggestions in Figure 3.4 to enable children to regulate their feelings and actions in order to increase productivity.

Figure 3.4. Developing Self-Regulation

○ **Help children find their strengths.** Assist them in recognizing their capabilities and their limitations. Be understanding. Consider together their concerns and their previous efforts and successes. Then help children set realistic goals for themselves. (More on goal setting in Chapter 10.)

○ **Teach skills.** Teach children good work habits, such as organizational skills, prioritizing, and how to approach tasks one
step at a time. This includes demonstrating how to gauge
the size and scope of a given task, and then how to go about
making time for it.

○ **Take five or ten—or more.** Encourage kids to take regular
short breaks and to make time for play and recreation, preferably outdoors if possible.

○ **Shelve the gadgetry.** Too many children spend inordinate
amounts of time with electronic devices, toys, or other things
that may distract them and that can be put aside temporarily.

○ **Give reasons.** Provide rationales for time limits, expectations,
and rules. If possible, set them together. Enable children to
understand why they have to complete something within a
certain block of time. Once respectful boundaries have been
set, be consistent with them.

○ **Praise the effort.** Offer direct, non-controlling, and positive
feedback. For example, a child may be asked to clean out the
birdcage, or clear his stuff from the hallway, or put away his
laundry before going to bed. If he does so, try reinforcing his
actions with the simple words "Thank you. I appreciate your
help." If he needs a reminder before retiring for the night,
perhaps say, "I'm sure you meant to follow through. Thanks
for taking the time now. I appreciate your help."

○ **Point the way.** Show children how to cope with disturbances.
Take a moment or two to review where he went off track, or
use the opportunity for a stretch, or to take a breather, or get
a refreshing snack.

○ **Pair feelings.** Show kids how to pair a good feeling with one
that is tougher to deal with as a way to provide perspective.
Guilt about not completing something can be piggybacked
with relief or joy that at least it has been started, and will
continue to be worked on.

○ **Make a contract.** Talk about commitment and what that means for the situation at hand. Work together to create a fair, doable, informal deal or "completion contract." Co-create a written document, co-sign and date it, and shake (or better still, hug) on the agreement. This can bolster a child's resolve, establish direction, and offset possible task avoidance.

○ **Find the prime time.** Help kids identify the times of day when they work best. For example when are they most energetic or less likely to be interrupted or distracted? Encourage them to use their prime time wisely.

○ **Teach pacing.** Show children how to pace their efforts. Real accomplishment often takes time and patience.

"How soon 'not now' becomes 'never.'"[41] Help children understand how to manage their successes, better understand possible failures, reduce stress, and self-regulate their feelings, actions, and productivity. All of these processes empower children to move forward so that *now* becomes doable—and *never* is no longer an issue.

CHAPTER 4

Procrastination and Young Children

"You don't have to see the whole staircase, just take the first step."

~ Martin Luther King

Children procrastinate differently at different ages, and the most common reasons for procrastination differ during various stages of children's lives. Kids of all ages procrastinate, and these behaviors range from puzzling to worrisome. Because every child is unique, and because sometimes the procrastination may be only a passing phase, the strategies of parents and teachers may change. The best approaches will vary depending on the child's age and maturity level.

This chapter focuses on procrastination tendencies in toddlers and young school-aged children. The next chapter deals with procrastinating tweens and adolescents. Of course, age range behaviors are not clear-cut, and sometimes behaviors that usually occur in younger children are seen in older kids, or vice versa. Plenty of younger kids *and* teens procrastinate when it comes time to cleaning their rooms, completing chores, or doing their schoolwork. Knowing something about child development at these different stages of life helps parents understand why their kids are procrastinating and, thus, what to do about it. While thinking about strategies, you will, of course, want to be flexible, sensitive, creative, and sensible. Many strategies will apply to children of any age or stage of development, regardless of which category you see them in here.

Toddlers

Little ones do procrastinate. They often have difficulty with tasks ranging from eating healthy foods to picking up blocks. They may not want to nap, eat their vegetables, help put away paints, or put on shoes and socks to get ready when adults want them to. The word *later* is very popular among the toddler set, and one they hear quite often from adults. What these one- to three-year-olds really mean is *no* or *not now*. They have only a loose concept of what *later* means because the idea of the future is vague, and they have not yet acquired time management skills. *Later* becomes a handy catchall, a distant place where punctuality and time don't really matter, like a far off Neverland of sorts.

Dr. Seuss wrote, "How did it get so late so soon? It's night before it's afternoon. December is here before it's June. My goodness how the time has flewn. How did it get so late so soon?"[42] On first reading, one would think this rhyme is written just for children, but think again. Developmentally, toddlers live very much in the present moment. They do not have a sense of what December or June is, let alone what lies in between. To them, time flying has something to do with wings.

It helps young children comprehend time if we put it into a context that they can understand. For example, they will grasp night as being dark and morning as being when they wake up with the sunlight. You can teach them what you mean when you say "After breakfast," or "Before bath-time," or "Once we reach Grandma's house." Small children who have a wayward attitude toward getting things done are not necessarily acting defiantly. They simply do not have a good sense of time, including what is early and what is late, how clocks and calendars figure into our daily routines, and why adults are so concerned about punctuality. Rhymes like the one above by Dr. Seuss, or *Hickory Dickory Dock*, *The Eeensy Weensy Spider*, and others are great for helping them understand the present and the future and about the sequence in which things happen. Also, we adults can often confuse the situation when we say *later* to children, when what we are really saying is "I've no intention of doing this, and I hope that you'll forget about it if I postpone it long enough."

Of course, *later* is not something one can actually see, touch, or fully experience in the present. There's *later* and there's even later—which may seem odd to young children. Like the fact that tomorrow never comes. Despite the confusion, young kids nevertheless often embrace *later* as a suitable time to do whatever it is they don't choose to do *now*.

Little children learn how to respond to the people in their world through their past experiences with them. Kiera likes to make a giant jumble with her blocks all over the kitchen floor. She knows that her mother will get angry, but her father will probably think it is no big deal. She knows that procrastinating with a particular cleanup is easier when the person looking after her is more blasé about it and not bothered by the mess. She already recognizes that certain situations result in different outcomes that she might get away with, depending on who's who and what's what. For example, her mother is intent on a set bath-time and bedtime routine, no two ways about it. And her father is unhappy when the tea party toys are left sitting on the dining room table where he often sits and does work. Kiera knows who accepts what, and when limits are strict and when they are simply suggestions.

When children have learned these tendencies, they will manipulate the situation simply because they have been allowed to behave that way in the past with little or no repercussions. In other words, we teach our children that procrastination is okay, at least in certain circumstances. Why should Kiera clean up the toys now when she can do it later? Better still, if she waits long enough, maybe someone else will do it for her.

Children learn responsibility when their parents establish basic rules and procedures with them, reinforce effort, show stick-to-itive-ness, and maintain that same standard with consistency. When a child masters dependability in one area, parents can gradually up the ante and steadily increase the degree of responsibility expected, e.g., "After you put the tea party dishes away, Kiera, please help me set the table for dinner." Children may seem reluctant at first, but they usually buy into the feelings of accomplishment that come with more responsibility, particularly if they are praised for it.[43]

Although preschool children generally have an *all about me* frame of reference, they often enjoy helping their parents and doing things for themselves. They can sense when others are proud, upset, or pleased. They also understand when they are the reason their parents are angry or happy—and whether completing things, or not completing them, might have something to do with that.

Parents can also teach kids to connect actions and feelings, e.g., "I'm a little sad because you haven't put away your crayons yet."[44] Emphasize that kids' actions and behaviors not only matter, but also that they are very important to working well together.

Kids get a handle on people and things by listening to what others say and by testing out ideas for themselves. This includes pushing boundaries. That is part of the learning process of every day life. We want to encourage children's thoughtful independence, and we also want them to learn new things by experimenting.

Toddlerhood is a time of discovery—of falling and getting back up again. A child's sense of self depends on a combination of factors such as previous experiences, feedback from parents and caregivers, and developmental maturity. Children thrive when given some autonomy within a relaxed, but safe and appropriately controlled, environment. So when toddlers say *no* or *not now*, they are test-driving their autonomy.

During these very early years, children are already actively trying to figure out the social aspects of life—whom to trust, what to try independently, and what steps to take in order to reach their goals. Children build their knowledge and sense of self by interacting with the world. Many social and cultural factors contribute to a child's sense of self, such as language, religion, nationality, family values, and educational opportunities.[45] As kids become more autonomous, they make mistakes and hopefully learn from the experiences and the consequences, including how to plan and prioritize. Whenever possible, we want them to decide not to procrastinate—not because we are hovering over them and urging them on, but because it makes sense to them.

This self-management applies to other behaviors as well. For example, Mason fusses and puts off having his afternoon nap. He becomes too exhausted to walk the four blocks to the park with his mother, and as a result he misses a chance to go on the swings and slides.

Yolanda does not want to put on her snowsuit and keeps squirming out of it. "Later," she says. But it starts getting dark at 4:30, and by the time she finally agrees, it's too dark to go out and build a snow fort. Toddlers can be taught that actions, such as procrastinating, lead to consequences, which can include missing out on what they would like to do. Parents can offer gentle reminders (but not lectures) about what has happened in the past as a result of procrastinating. Mason did not get to go to the park. Yolanda lost her chance to play in the snow. Children learn better from experiencing natural, logical consequences than they do from lectures or arbitrary punishments.[46] When these natural consequences occur, it also allows parents to be genuinely sympathetic, rather than scolding and punitive, e.g., "I'm sorry that your favorite toy was left outside and was rained on. What can you do to make sure that doesn't happen again?" This would be much more effective than, "Didn't I tell you to bring in your toys last night? See what happens when you procrastinate! You never listen to me."

When a young child postpones a task and steadfastly, perhaps defiantly, stands his ground, what are parents to do? First, think, rather than do. Is this an occasional occurrence or a recurring scene? Are stand-offs and put-offs becoming routine? Is there generally an understandable reason for the procrastination—such as the child feeling too tired, too hungry, too afraid, or too uncertain about what to do? What can parents do to help him avoid reluctance?

While occasional procrastination may yield to a little encouragement on the spot, a *pattern* of postponements is often more difficult to deal with. A child who delays putting away the playdough day after day after day, and is allowed to do so, finds it harder to get back into a more acceptable routine. (And the playdough gets hard and dried out, an ideal learning opportunity!)

Kids may not *want* to do something, and they may not appreciate why they should *have* to do it—just because someone else says so. This is not surprising; think about how you feel when you have to do something just because you're told to. We all appreciate some rationale as to why it makes sense to do a task now.

Recognize and pay careful attention to children's attitudes, influences, preferences, skills, and behaviors. Children vary tremendously in their temperaments, their processing speed, and their most productive time of day. Some may be feeling discouraged, over-whelmed, or rebellious.

Of course, sometimes a parent must insist on immediate compliance, especially if there are health or safety issues—sunscreen, helmets, and life jackets, come to mind. Obstinance and power struggles can be quite challenging, as most parents of two-year-old children can confirm.[47] Little ones may want to be in control of things, but they are not mature enough to understand the potential danger. Sometimes giving a choice is all that is needed. For example, "Would you like to put the sunscreen on your arms and then your face, or would you rather start with your face?" or, "Would you like the red life jacket or the blue one?" That way, they have some freedom and choice, but within the limits you have set. The really important behaviors are not open to negotiation.

Underlying all of this is a most important aspect—the relationship with the child. Children are more likely to comply with our requests if we have a strong, positive relationship with them. Young children who do not form strong relationships with others lack the opportunities to learn from role-models who can show them safe, responsible behavior and good work habits. Solid relationships that contribute to a child's development and well-being are those in which the adults in his life are attuned to his needs, support his capacities for learning and self-direction, and connect warmly, providing a sense of closeness. Encouragement, reinforcement, and gentle discipline are also part of the equation. All of this enables young children to get past the me-oriented focus of toddlerhood and learn how to function in the context of the wider world. There they will encounter endless influences and distractions, and they will discover that other people's desires, expectations, and beliefs may differ markedly from theirs. For example, to a three-year-old, dumping all the pieces from five puzzles into one big box may seem like a good idea (and requires less effort than getting five separate containers), but having to sort the many pieces out afterward is not something that she, her parents, or older siblings will likely relish. The three-year-old may not anticipate or appreciate the difficulty of the sorting task that lies ahead.

Think about what it is like to read a textbook on a difficult topic or one that you know very little about. Quantum physics, perhaps? Or imagine you have to play a complicated piece of music even though you are just a beginning pianist. It would be extremely challenging. In some ways, being a toddler is just like that. Every day you see and are asked to do numerous things you may not fully understand. This includes being savvy about time management and tasks that others ask you to do. Sometimes these tasks may even seem scary. (Like having to actually *talk* about quantum physics, or play that complicated music *in front of others*.)

As children acquire a basis of knowledge, they learn and remember. Learning is a process of construction no matter how old you are. Since most of us procrastinate when faced with tasks we are unsure of, one way to solve procrastination among preschoolers is to present things to them in a clear and simple fashion so they can process the information readily and build on knowledge and tasks that they have already mastered.

Help children make connections between what they already know and what you want them to know, then build from there. Focus on what is important, one thing at time. Too often we forget to do this, and we find ourselves giving a series of requests that seem simple to us, but which may feel overwhelming, unreasonable, or irrelevant to a preschooloer. Give them time to practice, and provide clues or reminders if there are signs of confusion. Help them understand the relevance of the tasks to their lives or to the functioning of the family, if at all possible. Be patient. Stay positive.

Figure 4.1. Teaching Toddlers to Prevent Procrastination

○ **Answer, explain, repeat.** Answer questions appropriately for the child's age. Reword the answer if necessary. Do not assume that kids know what to do because someone went over it already. They sometimes need to be told or shown things repeatedly.

○ **Have some fun.** Use word games, rhymes, puzzles, melodies, stories, stickers, or colorful visuals. A stuffed animal's experience with socks and shoes can mirror a child's procrastination. For example, "Lax the Lion was lyin' around. He couldn't go for a walk with his buddies because he didn't want to put on his shoes. Let's show the lion how it's done. Come sit on the floor. We'll put on your socks and shoes, and roar!" Pictures of a story or a series of events can be revisited or redrafted again and again.

○ **Encourage.** Praise small steps. They will lead to bigger ones. Praise effort. It leads to a positive mindset, and more effort.

○ **Be clear.** Make sure what is being asked of the child is reasonable for his age and ability. Give and take; compromise is a good lesson to learn.

○ **Organize.** Provide what is needed. For example, label or color-code storage containers for different toys if tidy-up time is a problem.

○ **Watch the clock.** If a child is learning to tell time, help her strengthen this skill with lots of opportunities to practice. Consider going out together to buy a special easy-to-read clock.

○ **Promote teamwork.** Doing things together with kids the first few times gives them the confidence to manage independently.

○ **Chunk the work.** Help toddlers organize by dividing the task into manageable chunks, e.g., "Let's pick up this side of the room now, and then we'll take a short break."

○ **Be positive.** Harsh criticism can escalate into a power struggle that can lead to increased procrastination. Give the child a way to save face by encouraging her to take just the first step. Shame can become another hurdle to overcome, one that can be avoided by supporting efforts as they occur.

○ **Take time out.** Model and take a break from doing, doing, doing. The key is balance and time management—which includes some free time.

Early Childhood

Children in the four- to ten-year-old bracket span several stages of development. They continue to learn in leaps and bounds. They question and want immediate and clear answers. They challenge. They still have strong self-interest. Like their younger counterparts, they want instant gratification. At the same time, they are also learning about empathy, hard work, morality, traditions, and many other subleties of life.

Most children at this age are in elementary school, in the process of developing a vast range of academic and interpersonal skills. They are learning to tell (and appreciate) time. They are less egocentric and more able to focus on others and their points of view. They think more logically and have begun to develop an understanding of abstract concepts, such as truth and honesty. They have a grasp of rules and limitations and why these mattter.

As Erik Erikson, a noted theorist in the area of personal development, suggested, development is a lifelong proess that takes place in a social context.[48] We learn from one another. For kids, school is an extremely important social context where they learn by interacting with others. Unfortunately, this can include learning to procrastinate.

According to Erikson, children in the age range of three to six take control of their actions and situations, along with a sense of purpose or of guilt. Then, from the ages of six to twelve, children acquire a sense of industry, productiveness, and conscientiousness—though some do not. A child who is successful at navigating schoolwork, goals, and so on, feels comptetent, whereas a child who is unsuccessful may develop feelings of inferiority. A student who experiences difficulty with spelling may balk at doing the assigned homework or participating in the weekly class spelling bee. The fear of not being able to keep up, or of possible embarrassment, may contribue to his reluctance and feelings of ineptitude.

What does this mean in practical terms? Parents and caregivers have to help children find a comfort zone where they can take control, learn to make decisions, and feel successful, both at home and school. Provide appropriate challenges and tasks for which kids can take responsibility. Give them choices (within limits) about books to read for recreation, extracurricular art projects, and homework scheduling.

Procrastination delays any possible accomplishment and can discourage a child from even trying again. Success leads to pride and to accomplishment, which gives them the confidence to keep going.

One thing *all* parents can do is to strengthen communication and links between home and school.[49] School is often where children experience their most daunting challenges, where they are likely to feel overwhelmed by tasks, and where they may procrastinate because they are unsure of themselves and their ability to manage those tasks. Parents need to understand the child's world and give importance to his perspectives. Do you listen attentively to what your kids have to say about their schooling? Don't just ask, "How was school today?" Instead, ask about their specific experiences:

"What did you learn?"

"What did you enjoy?"

"What was challenging?"

"What would you be interested in exploring further? That's interesting; why?"

If your child feels comfortable in talking with you about his school life, you will be much more likely to discover not only your child's organizational approaches to schoolwork and other tasks, but also in which areas he may need help.

Keep in touch with teachers. Be accessible to meet with them, respond promptly to any messages or questions, check the school's website regularly, and become active in the educational community by joining committees, participating in events, or helping out as a volunteer or in a mentorship program.[50] Knowing that you are in close touch with the teacher will give pause to kids who might otherwise be inclined to develop excuses for putting off their schoolwork, like "But Mrs. Kenway said the assignment doesn't have to be done till sometime next month," or "We don't have any tests coming up." Parents who stay involved know timelines and learning expectations, and are able to see the school picture for themselves, which can affect how smoothly things go at home. (See Chapter 6 for a discussion on children's different academic achievement levels.)

Sometimes, of course, children complain to their parents saying things like, "You're always looking over my shoulder! Nobody else's parents are like that!" Calmly and simply reply (and repeat, if necessary), "I stay involved because I love you, and because it's important for me to know what's going on at school."

Each learning environment—classroom, sports team, art studio, or elsewhere—has its own particular dynamic. Strong communication networks between home and these other settings help children succeed, and teamwork is key to this success. This calls for open, respectful discourse and mutually developed and understood expectations. Both sides need to know about children's feelings, learning needs, and work habits. Adults who work together can be more consistent in their encouragement, guidance, and problem solving. In today's fast-paced world, it is often difficult to find the time and energy to reach out repeatedly to a child's teachers, but if procrastination problems can be solved early in a child's life, there will be fewer of these problems later.

Rita Emmett, a motivational speaker, consultant, and author, has some simple, doable solutions geared for procrastinators of any age, and she suggests using acronyms as memory aids.[51] Here are a couple of her tips. The first is for kids who feel overwhelmed, and the second has to do with time management.

*Take the **STING** out of feeling overwhelmed:*
Select one task you've been putting off.
Time yourself. Give the task one full hour.
Ignore everything else. Focus on doing just this one task.
No breaks allowed.
Give yourself a reward when the job is done.

*Tips to share with your child to help clear that **BUSY** calendar:*
Be selective; prioritize your activities; choose your battles.
Use a calendar to block out "Catch up days."
Set limits; pause, breathe, slow down.
Yes can get you in trouble; learn to say no.

Of course, many children have already mastered the art of saying *no.* Others use the words *I can't,* when what they really mean is *I won't.* Talking about the difference between these two phrases makes for a useful discussion.[52] Whether it is getting down to the task of prioritizing, completing an assignment, or something else altogether, kids are likely to need encouragement and assistance.

Figure 4.2 gives some more ideas to help elementary school-aged children conquer the inclination to procrastinate.

Figure 4.2. Helping Young School-Aged Children Fight Procrastination

○ **Monitor and adjust.** Keep watch over the child's progress and change tactics when necessary. It is better to have more ideas to stay on task than he has to keep procrastinating.

○ **Is it engaging?** Children are less likely to procrastinate when a task is enjoyable and they feel comfortable. Think carefully about program placement and challenge levels.

○ **Buddy up.** Work with the child's teacher early on to co-create an action plan, with a sensible timeline, workable guidelines, and considerations for everyone involved. Advocating for a child takes collaboration, effort, planning, and follow-through.[53]

○ **Goal!** Show children how to set manageable, reachable goals—ones that are doable and spark interest. Aim for one attainable step at a time. Talk out loud as you plan so children can hear.

○ **Feeling good**. Chat about how people feel once a task is completed. Discuss and help children understand different emotions often associated with procrstination (such as guilt and regret) and also feelings asscociated with accomplishment (such as happiness and pride).

○ **Bump up the vocabulary.** Introduce words like *intentions*, *consequences*, *avoidance,* and *productivity*. Many kids enjoy taking ownership of and then actually using big words.

○ **Teach pacing.** It is sensible to pause at intervals when completing a task, to take a break and make sure everything is on track. This time-out lets children recoup from dealing with time frames or other pressures.

○ **Pick your battles.** Some have to be dealt with immediately (for example, those that are safety-related or pose a serious detriment to others) and others are less pressing. Should you react? Wait? Ignore? Remember, children learn when they have to face the consequences of their actions, or rather, inactions.

○ **Convey confidence.** Motivate kids by instilling the confidence to begin a task—encouraging them to make that first move required to make things happen. Reiterate the importance of saying to oneself, "I'm ready, I can do it, let's go!"[54]

○ **Use the clock.** Help kids learn to tell time, including how to use a 24-hour clock, which can be fun to learn. Let them play with and become familiar with a timer. Don't foist it on kids, but co-develop some creative applications for procrastination-related circumstances, e.g., "Pick three colored pencils, then flip the timer and see if you can do three of those homework questions before the rainbow sand runs out."

○ **Encourage collaboration.** Play groups or interest groups (like clubs, teams, or scouting) give kids opportunities to become excited about doing things with others. Talking about activities and working together can also help.

○ **Be patient.** Show sensitivity as kids learn to navigate new situations, time-frames, and challenges.

○ **Finally, don't procrastinate on getting involved!** Try these strategies.

CHAPTER 5

Procrastination and Older Children

"The moment where you doubt whether you can fly, you cease forever being able to do it."

~ J. M. Barrie, in *Peter Pan*

A particularly challenging time often occurs when children approach adolescence. They often resist taking on additional responsibilities, including assignments and chores. How can parents help these kids become more industrious? This chapter is loosely divided into two age categories, tweens (or preteens) and teenagers.

Tweens

As kids reach preadolescence, it is increasingly important that parents continue to develop and maintain strong connections between home and school so that they can be staunch advocates for their children's aspirations and learning needs.

Often, however, tweens do not want their parents to be so involved with what is happening; they are trying to assert their independence, and understandably so. Certainly, tweens have an important and increased responsibility to become more self-reliant, to have faith in their abilities, and to invest in their own learning, connecting it to their ambitions and to what is going on in their lives. Nevertheless, parents need to provide a safety net, although they can increasingly pull the net back as warranted and as their kids show increased self-management skills. A key part of managing the safety net wisely is for parents to continue to be in close communication with teachers.

Preteens are clearly old enough to understand how their behavior contributes to their advancement or problems at school, and to their ease or difficulties at home. Hopefully, they have also learned to be fair-minded and respectfully assertive, and to use their interests and strengths as gateways to new and exciting ventures. When activities or learning tasks are personally motivating, kids become engaged and less likely to procrastinate.

Motivation involves creating and harnessing momentum, and parents and teachers can spark kids' interests in many ways to make tasks more enticing. At a basic level, motivators might include applause or a favorite treat. At a more sophisticated level, motivators might be exciting choices or developing challenging but realizable goals. The bottom line is to make an activity meaningful. Remember, too, that expectations are more readily met when tasks and ability level match. Parents can advocate for suitable learning matches for their kids.[55]

A good way to motivate another person is to be flexible about how you present the task, being careful to consider the pacing, structure, focus, and feedback. Respect the unique qualities of the individual.[56] Chat about possibilities, co-create an approach, think about how to make an activity fun, and share ideas with one another. Most importantly, and especially where kids are concerned, bolster their self-esteem. Encourage their expectations of success ("You know you can do it!"); appreciate their efforts ("You've gotten off to a great start!"); and reinforce the value and relevance of the task ("Learning to do this will make the next step so much easier!"). You'll find a lot more information on motivation in Chapter 11, including strategies you can use to help motivate kids throughout the early years and into young adulthood.

Tweens are not little children, nor are they full-fledged adolescents. They are caught in between, and for some individuals, that in itself can present a challenge. Although various stages of cognitive and child development may appear to be separate, the many changes kids go through occur as more of a continuous or gradual progression. Each child advances at his or her own rate.[57]

Most preadolescents are able to reason logically. This includes being able to transfer thought to action and goal-directed behavior. They can work through a series of steps much better than when they were younger, e.g., "I have to do this, and this, and then that." Then they can mentally reverse the steps to go back to the starting point and configure a plan. However sometimes, especially if the plan seems too complicated or unappealing, they will decide to opt out. I recently saw a poster of the Cookie Monster that read, "Today I will live in the moment, unless it's unpleasant in which case I will eat a cookie."

Living in the moment is what lots of kids do. Nevertheless, the ability to plan and delay gratification is important for managing procrastination and factors into a person's success in various aspects of life years later. In the early 1970s, psychologist Walter Mischel conducted the Stanford Marshmallow experiments. This classic series of studies has received a great deal of attention over several decades.[58] Each child was given an opportunity to choose between accepting an immediate reward (such as a marshmallow, pretzel, or cookie), or waiting till the experimenter returned (after approximately 15 minutes) and then receiving two rewards. The researchers were investigating the power of self-control and children's ability to live in the future moment, rather than the present one. Follow-up studies suggested that children who were able to wait for the rewards tended to have better lives, as measured by various factors such as educational attainment, professional success, health, and the ability to sustain relationships. The studies have generated considerable interest and also controversy, including whether such a test of children three to five years of age is really an indicator of patience and impulse control in the long term.[59]

But what does this have to do with procrastination, and how does it relate to preteens? As children mature and gain experience of the world around them, they better understand the benefits of planning ahead, prioritizing, and maintaining focus. Even adults often react to the seemingly urgent (like a phone call or text message from a friend), rather than the truly important (like driving the car and keeping eyes on the road, not on some electronic device).[60]

Younger people tend to focus on living in the present. The fallout is that middle- or long-term planning may not be their idea of a good time, nor appear to be a necessity. After all, short-term events may seem demanding, too. What's the rush? Everyone procrastinates. They have seen their parents put things off. Renowned and successful experts, even professional planners and organizers, delay action.[61] What kids may not realize—in part because they lack experience and may not be thinking broadly—is that inaction translates to missed opportunities. Punctuality? "Eh, not so important." Time management? "Tomorrow." The future? "Who knows what it'll bring? Whatever." If the here and now is gratifying and something else may not be, then the *status quo* has the upper hand.

No one can predict the future, but we can help tweens (and younger children, too) understand that there are costs and balances in life. They can be encouraged to talk about what leads to accomplishment and success, as well as what thwarts it, and they can explore online resources on the subject and initiate conversations themselves.[62] Sharing experiences links people together, and their identities grow, develop, and change in the process. When children's and teenagers' identities are supported and reaffirmed it contributes to their self-esteem.

A child's identity is shaped by what she is exposed to, including people, learning, and travel. Children construct knowledge as they act upon and interact with the world. As with any group of kids, there is considerable diversity. Something relevant to children is meaningful to them. Something that is stimulating, thought provoking, or appropriately challenging is likely to be enticing. On the other hand, if things are not interesting, applicable, or pertinent, then why bother with them? Parents can help kids understand what is expected of them and why it is reasonable, why it is important, and why it will be useful. If there is an element of choice and some creativity or fun to be had, so much the better. Stretching oneself and then feeling the gratification and pride of accomplishment may be the best motivator of all.

As kids begin to develop a clearer sense of self, their past accomplishments become guideposts for the future. Granted, not everything in life is bright lights and enticement. Realistically, preadolescence consists of many ups and downs. Cognitively, physically, emotionally, and socially, they are very much still emerging. As they confront changes, meet new people, make mistakes, strive to fit in, and yet be true to themselves, they will find that every day, every encounter, every experience is different. And, in the context of all of that, parents and teachers have expectations for them at home, school, and elsewhere. What should they tackle first? What can they afford to put off until later? They have chores, homework assignments, and commitments. Preadolescence can be strenuous.

Parents must respect kids' "personal capital." That is, who they are and what they bring to the family, to their learning environments, to their relationships with others, and to their daily experiences. Their capabilities and efforts may be strong and well intentioned, but at the same time, they can be affected by everything else that goes into the hard and ongoing work of maturing. Technologies have increased the speed of production. Complex events unfold and often raise difficult questions about society. Simple stop-and-smell-the-roses pleasures seem to be less prevalent. Kids are juggling all of this and more, and are doing so without the benefit of the experience and maturity that adults possess.

When parents badger their children to get down to work, it often goes in one ear and out the other. Parents can make an effort to pay attention to the messages they may intentionally or unintentionally convey through their choice of words when speaking with kids and referring to their behaviors. Parents who say about their daughter, "She's always distracted!" could in fact be misconstruing her ability because she is able to multitask. Other parents may think their tween is defiant, saying, "He refuses do anything I ask of him!" However, he could be determined and working to get through demands in his own way. A preadolescent described by his parents as "achingly slow at doing things" could actually be deliberately and thoughtfully engaged. Kids who develop ways of functioning that work for them do not appreciate it when parents label their actions, nag endlessly, or assume they are using defensive ploys or copping out.

When that happens, kids may not know how to express themselves or how to explain their reasons for acting as they do. Parents who misinterpret their children's actions may also miss opportunities for fruitful discussion. Kids who feel misunderstood or maligned can respond in various ways, such as clamming up, becoming indignant, or procrastinating further. (Remember the Rebel persona?) Others may develop learned helplessness, characterized by not wanting to tackle challenges or anything new. "If that's what my parents think, I might as well give up,"—and as such the child might lose self-confidence, shut down, and avoid a task (like the Doubter).

Parents can reinforce more positive behaviors by reinforcing their kid's efforts and by helping kids take pleasure in doing whatever they can. Success can be put in the context of initiative and progress as opposed to some final product. Parents should keep an open mind about what might underlie their child's procrastination, and stay alert for times when they can strengthen channels of communication with their tween. This includes finding out what really matters to them, and why.

Kids tend to prioritize based on what is relevant to them. Some things will be deemed important and will be tended to promptly, whether or not their parents see it as top priority. Others tasks will be postponed or ignored. If something is left undone or put aside for another day, there may be consequences to pay. But sometimes that's okay. That's how kids learn. They have to know they can pick themselves up and get going again. Parents who step in and cajole (or yell, demean, bribe, or take over and do whatever needs doing for them) are not helping matters. Parents who rescue their kids are also not doing them a favor, e.g., "You didn't bring home the form I was supposed to sign? I better rush right over to the school and look after it!" versus, "You didn't bring home the form I was supposed to sign? I guess you'll have to speak to the teacher about that." Natural consequences become learning opportunities.[63]

Parents can be respectful of kids' burgeoning lives, help them prioritize intelligently, offer guidance without being controlling, and demonstrate how to complete tasks one step at a time. As a result, parents are likely to find encounters with their tweens less stressful, with fewer stand-offs. Thoughtful and patient direction within the complexity of kids' lives can make all the difference in whether they will make smart decisions about what to do with the 24 hours they have each day. Like the rest of us, they appreciate support, understanding, and encouragement.

Figure 5.1. Working with Tweens to Manage Procrastination

○ **Use self-talk.** Teach kids to talk themselves through the steps of a task.[64] This cognitive self-instruction is not babyish; adults do it all the time when driving, following a recipe, or when clarifying or working through a series of demands, e.g., "I'm going to sort through that mountain of laundry, then put the first batch in the washer, and after that I'll reward myself with a cup of tea." Self-talk can be helpful for organization and self-regulation, especially when a person starts getting bogged down. Parents can introduce and explain this process. (Tip: Pick an opportune time and keep it concise.)

○ **Find new perspectives.** Chat with kids about other peoples' perspectives. Discuss how others (teachers, classmates, etc.) count on them to complete things and that it is not fair when tasks are left undone and people are stuck waiting. This is not to inspire a sense of guilt, but rather a sense of responsibility.

○ **"Sorry" is not a strategy.** Apologizing for recurring procrastination that somehow affects others is all well and good, but after a while, requests for forgiveness begin to wear thin. Parents can help kids understand that being sorry about inappropriate behavior is best indicated with action that remedies the situation, such as putting forth the required effort for a group assignment or doing a timely review of material for an upcoming collaborative presentation.

○ **Track progress.** Things are more straightforward when goals are specific and people can gauge their progress. Parents can help kids see and appreciate their interim accomplishments as they work through a task.

○ **Allow independence in priorities.** Identity development can be a fragile process. Keep this in mind and give a little leeway as a child discovers his way, even if that includes a compulsion to put some things off in lieu of others that seem more important at a given point in time. When a child says, "I'll clean my room *after* I finish checking this out…" It may be NHL hockey trades, a new book, earthquake indicators, political unrest, or something else that matters a good deal to the child.

○ **Ask around.** Touch base with other parents and find out what sorts of strategies they use when their kids procastinate. Share ideas, including unusual or innovative ones.

○ **Encourage grit.** Use meltdowns as teachable moments. Help kids understand that we all have times when we get upset and that we all make mistakes. Talk about resilience and how wrangling success from failure is a learning process. Kids *can* find the fortitude necessary to keep going when responsibilities or demands become taxing.[65]

○ **Link self-discipline to others.** Teach children about self-discipline, what it means and how it contributes to their success as a student, family member, and friend—three very different realms. Specifc examples are much more meaningful than generalities. Instead of, "Show some reliability!" try saying, "If you start that assignment today, I'm sure your group members will appreciate it."

○ **Use checklists.** Help kids learn to develop checklists for tasks so they can track their progress. This can be gratifying, which can provide momentum. Sometimes a task seems overwhelming, but breaking it into subtasks and charting progress makes it less daunting. Small steps can lead to great change: "It's better to take many small steps in the right direction than to make a great leap forward only to stumble backward."[66]

○ **Do the math.** Suggest that kids do the math. How much time are they wasting?[67] How much time are they using productively? Daily? Weekly? Let kids figure out the ratio and implications. Encourage them to chat about how to use time wisely. Thinking and talking about this may help kids feel more accountable for their productivity.

Adolescents

Do you remember your own teenage years? What is memorable about them? What influenced *your* adolescent development? Teens are a work in progress, on the cusp of adulthood. They confront many external influences—social, cultural, familial, academic, and more. Each person has unique experiences.

A person's drives, abilities, beliefs, decisions, values, experiences, and personal history all factor into their identity.[68] A teenager is in the process of establishing individuality. This can involve experimenting with possible identities, investigating alternative lifestyles, exploring causes, and taking risks. Adolescence can also be a time for rebellion. Teenagers want independence and do not like being told what to do or when to do it. When parents nag or try to enforce arbitrary rules, it may only intensify rebellion. In the rebellious behavior department, procrastination is not nearly as serious as other forms of jockeying for independence, so parents have to be careful to keep things in perspective. One way to do this is to allow teens to make choices (even if their judgment is not ideal), and if consequences are hard to reconcile, to help kids find their way. Focus and comment on their responsible behaviors, letting them know that you are aware of their efforts and appreciate that they want some autonomy.

Teens are curious creatures, independent yet peer-driven, both defiant and compliant, sometimes leaders, and sometimes followers. Social relationships are increasingly important. Teenagers are impressionable, wanting to know what their peers and other people are doing. They expect parents and teachers to trust them more. They prefer to set their own rules, and whether or not they choose to follow them. They are not always easy to track, and it seems to be their mission to keep parents on their toes.

Erik Erikson's theory of psychosocial development describes individuals' accomplishments at different stages of life, and he calls adolescence a time of identity versus role confusion.[69] As teens develop a sense of identity, they make deliberate choices about what they will act upon, what they will tolerate, and what they will disregard, set aside, or reject. This applies to schoolwork and various responsibilities, as well as to personal commitments to ideas and people. How teenagers feel about personal explorations and commitments shapes their productivity.

Parents can give teens opportunities to learn about others' accomplishments and recommend resources as they work through the perplexing aspects of their evolving identities. Friends, family, neighbors, teachers, and community members can all be role models. Teens notice the values and behaviors of the adults in their lives and reject or admire what they see.[70] This applies to work ethics, resilience, self-confidence, and more. Kids who need help in these areas might benefit from a chat with school guidance personnel or community-based counselors.

Adolescence is a good age for developing career awareness, including how careers involve differing amounts of education and eventual pay. Parents can provide kids with insights, offer recommendations for educational programs, and suggest career options. When adolescents recognize their strengths and feel comfortable in their own skin they are more likely to develop self-assurance, follow their pursuits, and commit to achieving their goals. In the whole scheme of things, finding one's true self is also a matter of being purposeful—that is, creating and seizing opportunities as they arise, and as time allows.

Teenagers sometimes seem to live in different time zones from everyone else. Why does it seem like they always want to stay up all night, every night (doing whatever), and sleep in endlessly? What is it about their internal clocks that makes them resist synchronizing with others?

Each of us can learn to recognize our own bodily rhythms. Recent studies have shown that teens concentrate best later in the day.[71] Many schools have changed start times to adjust to the fact that teens have trouble starting school too early. Rescheduling a task from morning to afternoon just might be a wise choice for a teen, forestalling procrastination.

Learning to recognize and harness one's natural rhythms can make a difference in productivity. For example, Tessa prefers to complete a task late at night rather than when her parent thinks she should. If the task gets done and she will not suffer from extreme sleep deprivation, then a bit of flexibility is fine. Parents can work toward being attuned to their teen's natural rhythms and to recognize fatigue. Perhaps chores, other repsonsibilities, and even homework can be completed at alternative and more effective times, and a discussion and flexibility about this may be beneficial.

Teenagers are old enough to appreciate and learn from thoughtful conversation and wise words of others. When parents or other adults share helpful advice (without lecturing or badgering), kids can apply this to their daily workloads and responsibilities. If they actually read about the advice themselves, they are more likely to try it out and apply it even more consciously and effectively. Parents can become familiar with books or other resources on productivity that might energize teenagers. Thought-provoking suggestions can help them better understand how to deal with demands and challenges. Indeed, time spent talking with adolescents about good books is time well spent.

By way of example, Sean Covey is the author of a book that kids might find interesting. He has written about seven habits for highly effective teenagers, and all of these habits are relevant for overcoming procrastination.[72] The first three are particularly useful for a discussion as teens move from dependence to independence.

Habit #1: Be proactive. Take responsibility for choices and consequences. This would include showing intitiative and a willingness to jump in and follow through with an eye toward what might happen as a result. No one can look into the future, but everyone can be anticipatory. Kids can learn to use foresight and to take responsibility for their actions and outcomes.

Habit #2: Begin with the end in mind. Have a vision or mission statement. People need to have a sense of where they are going to move ahead. Have an action plan—those are two very important words. The first implies movement and progress, and the second preparation.

Habit #3: Put first things first. Plan and prioritize based on importance. Sometimes kids need help recognizing what is important and what is not. They should know what to address first, then next, and next.

The next four habits have to do with getting along with others. This connectivity is especially applicable to teenagers who, as they mature, will have to learn about interdependence in order to accomplish their goals.

Habit #4: Focus on a win-win scenario. Work with others to find what is mutually respectful and beneficial in order to get things done. When kids collaborate and share ideas, they inspire and propel one another forward. Procrastination is less likely when they know that others are depending upon them to do their fair share.

Habit #5: Seek first to understand and then to be understood. This involves caring, openmindedness, and reciprocal listening and communication. These are fundamental to relationship-building, leadership development, and accomplishment.

Habit #6: Synergize. People should capitalize on their strengths and tap into the strengths of others. Kids who know they are prone to procrastinate can ask others to encourage them and help keep them on track. It's good to work together.

The final habit, #7: Sharpen the saw. By this, Covey refers to balance and renewal in various forms. This includes relaxing, finding resources, and continually seeking to refresh and improve oneself. It is about equilibrium, determining what a person can do for himself, and how he can connect with others in ways that will stimulate personal growth.

Kids who think about these seven habits will be better prepared and able to steer themselves in constructive ways, at home, at school, and in the community.

As they are working their way through high school, adolescents think about many things, such as relationships and what their peers are up to. However, thoughts of college or work experience opportunities are often also on their minds. Realistically, this train of thought can get easily get derailed by tasks that generate procrastination. Teenagers have to decide which institutions or work settings to apply to, and that requires considerable information gathering, involving both time and effort. Applications have to be submitted by certain deadlines, and filling them out can be stressful and complicated. Applicants have to clarify instructions, respond to questions, write short essays and cover letters, compile references, and plow through assorted material. And if a deadline is missed, that's that. All of this can weigh very heavily on teenagers who already feel inundated with demands—and it can be especially difficult for those who have a tendency to procrastinate. Parents can talk with their kids about devising a plan with specific timelines for completing the many and varied aspects of application procedures.

Parents can also help their kids work through the process of applying to colleges and other post-secondary possibilities by encouraging an early start. Researching options while still in freshman and sophomore high-school years will allay some of the pressure. In addition to searching schools online, parents can look for "college nights" that are organized in cities throughout the country; here, teens can collect information and talk to college recruiters.[73] Parents and kids can put together a collection of folders with information about schools of higher learning that are of particular interest, including prerequisite courses, due dates, important contacts, and so on. Organized documentation helps kids feel more in control of what might lie ahead.[74]

Parents can use gentle reminders and encouragement, such as "I see the college applications folder on your desk. It's great that you're getting started on these and that you've remembered that some of the deadlines are just two weeks away." You have succeeded in conveying a positive nudge in the right direction, without nagging.

Finally, consider broaching a discussion about consequences by asking, "What will happen if...?" For example, what will be the costs of not completing an application? What if the submission deadline is missed? Better understanding of requirements and consequences comes about when kids use strategies involving reflection, organization, and long-term planning. Sometimes extra lead time is necessary.

Lastly, teenagers benefit from seeing their parents learn how to improve their own behavioral tendencies. For example, reading a book on something they need to brush up on (maybe becoming more tolerant and, ahem, understanding of procrastination). This demonstrates that regardless of age, there's no time like the present to embark on strategies for improvement.

Figure 5.2. Working with Adolescents to Confront Procrastination

○ **Be open-minded.** Value and respect the teen's viewpoints—as long as she is not damaging to herself or to others.

○ **Focus on the behavior.** Separate the off-task behavior from the person. Teenagers may be in the process of trying out different roles and options as they form their identities. Focus on addressing the *behavior*, which may include tendencies to procrastinate on specific assignments or other responsibilities, without criticizing the *individual*.

○ **Connect skills and careers.** Parents can help schools organize careeer days, where students listen to people representing various careers. Starting in the pre-teen years, parents can talk with kids about the huge variety of careers in all fields, so teens see that interests, areas of strength, and school performance can lead to successful careers. For instance, if math is a strength, consider what careers involve math—engineering, science, computer science, architecture, construction, etc. What careers require strong language skills? Journalism, law, freelance writing, editing, broadcasting, etc. And so on.

○ **Respect privacy.** Respect the teen's privacy if he doesn't want to share his feelings about his workload. He may be more open about his concerns or emotions at another point in time.

○ **Connect values and actions.** Help teenagers recognize inconsistencies between their values and any actions they take. For example, they may realize it is a smart idea to enlist the support of others to handle an overwhelming, stressful, boring, or confusing situation, but still refuse to ask for help.

○ **Celebrate successes when they happen.** Be positive. Appeal to the individual's maturity and her ability to comprehend the distinction between right and wrong, early and late, reliable and irresponsible.

○ **Teen coaching can offer clarity.** Adolescents can learn the value of seeing things through to completion while in the process of coaching younger kids.

○ **Don't pester.** Parents become exasperated and teens tune them out. It makes more sense to review and adopt some context-specific strategies for ending procrastination. (See Chapter 9 for recurring issues like messiness, chores, and homework completion.)

○ **Be creative.** An occasional non-embarrasing sticky note or card may do the trick.

○ **Keep it real.** Encourage kids to set realistic expectations and timelines for themselves.

○ **Age does not equal competence.** Although teens can do many things younger children cannot, do not assume that competence is predicated upon age.

CHAPTER 6
School Daze and Procrastination

"We cannot do everything at once, but we can do something at once."

~ Calvin Coolidge

Procrastination occurs particularly often at school, though not necessarily in all areas. Students often delay, dally, and defer in areas where they have difficulty. Some children and teenagers struggle in one or more academic areas, and so their achievement levels may not be consistent from one subject to another. One student might forge ahead working out statistics, but procrastinate when it comes to assigned reading. Other students may be especially industrious and timely when it comes to music, art, leadership activities, or sports. Procrastination particularly happens when a task is not enjoyable, such as when kids are given new or demanding assignments that are overly challenging.

Optimally, the pace and depth of schoolwork should match a child's ability levels and interests; otherwise, the likelihood of motivational problems and task avoidance increases.[75] Kids with academic difficulties may not be receiving the assistance they need to stay focused and to avoid procrastination. Similarly, gifted learners—those working well beyond their age or grade peers in some areas—may require advanced or specially targeted educational opportunities. Parents can speak to teachers about matching the school program to the child's areas of strength and weakness, interests, and learning preferences, as well as strategies to keep him engaged. Although some parents are reluctant, thinking that the teachers don't want their involvement, in actuality most teachers greatly appreciate the opportunity to work jointly with parents in this way. Assessments of various sorts are available and can help match a child's educational experiences with his particular learning needs.[76]

When considering assessment of children's cognitive capabilites, remember that tests are not infallible measures of what someone can do, nor are they predictors of future success. Although they are helpful in providing standardized measures, tests are shorthand devices for what parents and teachers can discern over time. Parents should take time to observe and reflect upon the multiple day-to-day signs of how their child is functioning. Other indicators include learning portfolios, teachers' daily assessments, and reports—all of which can contribute to a thoughtful review of the experiences and factors that lead to learning outcomes and overall well-being.[77] Differing capacities can affect procrastination tendencies. Whether or not a child needs special assistance, his academic ability level can have an impact on his productivity.

Special Needs Learners

Some kids find that daily expectations and the ongoing demands of dealing with one activity after another are just too hard to handle. Others may have problems adapting to major changes, such as moving to a new neighborhood or school, or experiencing a loss in the family. Inadequate sleep, poor nutrition, substance abuse, depression, bullying, or friendship concerns can prompt procrastination behaviors and underachievement. Certainly, there are many different reasons why children may struggle with schoolwork, and often difficulties can be overcome once parents and teachers figure out the underlying reason for the behavior.

Although the focus of this book is not on accommodating the many and varied special education needs of individuals, parents should recognize that a child's problems with self-regulation, achievement, and behavior may stem from issues that fall under the special education umbrella. If, for example, a child exhibits impulsivity, restlessness, distractibility, and mood changes, and you are worried about this, then meet with your child's teacher to talk about what to do. It may also make sense to speak with the pediatrican or with your family physician.[78] You may decide to have your child assessed at the school or by a recommended licensed professional within your community. When thinking about all of this, parents should ask themselves (and the teacher) what useful information is needed so that everyone can work together to better understand and effectively attend to any specific needs.[79]

Sometimes procrastination is a result of school difficulties, but in other cases a child struggles at school because he is a victim of his own procrastination—putting things off, not focusing on assignments, making excuses for work left to languish in a desk drawer, etc. As a result, he ends up compomising his productivity and achievement levels. Procrastination may be a child's response to his perception that he is unable to meet expectations. This could be because of a lack of skill sets, inappropriate programming, excessive demands, power struggles with parents, peer pressures, or something else altogether. He thinks he cannot do something, so he avoids trying.

Every child needs to have his sense of self-worth reinforced, but this is particularly relevant for children with special learning needs. Additionally, kids need to learn to trust themselves and to value their own capabilities. Parents can encourage this by helping children appreciate the satisfaction of *doing*, as opposed to *avoiding*.

Ben, one of the students in Miss Gilroy's class, procrastinated because he was unsure how to do an assignment. He avoided the work because he did not feel confident about how to approach it and decided he would wait for a better time to begin. However, when exactly is a "better" time? Later? Too much later, and he could end up falling farther and farther behind.

Teachers sometimes use the word *scaffolding* to describe assistance given to children who need additonal help or support. Just like the scaffolding on a house which gives workers support to reach difficult spots as they build, parents and teachers can offer surer footing and guidance to help children structure their learning. And like the scaffolding on a building, this help is meant to be temporary; once the work can stand on its own, the scaffolding comes down. Scaffolding can take many forms. Examples include clarifying instructions, providing a sample response, checking work after just one or two items have been attempted, demonstrating what needs tweaking, encouraging careful review of notes, and working alongside a child at the outset of a task while gradually letting him take ownership of it. When kids feel frustrated, they will be reluctant to take a first step, let alone a second or third. "Scaffolding" those initial steps gives children a foothold and a sense of success and competence from which they can continue to build, often on their own.

When kids procrastinate because they feel unable to perform, they need a boost to their self-efficacy—that is, the belief a person has about her own ability to do something. Students with high self-efficacy trust that they are capable of succeeding, and so they are more likely to take on challenging tasks.[80] Students with low self-efficacy tend to be more reluctant. Self-efficacy develops from previous successes, which can often be specific to a particular academic area. For example, a student may have high self-efficacy in math and lower self-efficacy in art or music. Kids are more inclined to start an assignment and then follow it to completion if they have experienced success in that area before, if they feel adept at the outset, and if they do not get stuck midway. However, if something is new or seems too difficult, a child may put it off because she sees it as a threat to her self-efficacy.

How can adults help children feel more successful? Try brainstorming unusual, creative, or less complicated ways to approach a task. Break the task into components and show kids how to set sub-goals that they can attain. Remind them that you believe in their abilities so they will come to believe in them, too. Encourage them to ask questions about what is expected of them, and let them know you are happy to answer. Have them maintain a log or portfolio of their achievements and remind them about past successes. So often people forget about their past successes and focus on the seemingly daunting new ones that they face. Give them opportunities to pair their weaknesses with their strengths. For example, a young child who enjoys drawing but is reluctant to work on her alphabet letters ("Too hard!") can be encouraged to see the letters as pictures. If parents take a creative approach and make the task enjoyable, she will be more interested in tackling it.

By building a record of success, children develop confidence, extend their capabilities, and become more motivated to get the job done.

Figure 6.1. Special Needs Learners: Managing Procrastination

○ **Don't interrupt.** Give kids some time and space when they are working their way through a task.

○ **Remember the four *R*s.** When kids falter, help them find a means to re-envision, repair, revise, or redo without feeling incompetent.

○ **Steer clear of competitive sitiuations.** Do not pit one child against another or highlight differences between them such that one feels inferior, or superior.

○ **Find resources.** If children lose momentum part way through a task or activity, help them find any additional information they may need.

○ **Visualize success.** Encourage kids to imagine successful completion and to think about how they are going to get there, e.g., "I *can* do that. I just have to work at this and this."

○ **Talk to teachers.** Chat together about how to develop sub-goals—that is, reasonable interim targets that will enable a child to see and measure his progress en route to an end goal. For example, answering one end-of-chapter question per evening over the course of several nights or clearing out one desk drawer every week until all the junk is gone and the remaining papers are in order.

○ **Join a study group.** Sometimes working with a group is the answer to greater productivity. This might mean providing kids with peer supports and a milieu in which they can push each other to work harder.

○ **Check the IEP.** An IEP is an Individual Education Plan that contains recommendations for instruction and programming. The plan is based on information acquired from assessment procedures. Not all students have an IEP. Parents can check with teachers to ensure that the educational plan is being followed and continue to monitor progress at home.

○ **Give extra consideration to transition times.** Any given day can be fast-paced, and children can encounter unexpected changes in their lives. For example, an unanticipated switch in academic programs or teachers, or an issue with friends. Give children the time and reassurance they may need both to understand changes and to adapt to them.

Average to Bright Learners – Activating Avoiders and Busting the Buts

Kids who are quite capable but choose to postpone things may do so for reasons that make sense to them—even though at first blush those reasons may not make sense to their parents. Perhaps you have heard your child say things like this: "It's already too late," or, "I promise I'll get to it tomorrow," or, "I have to finish something else first." Kids come up with endless excuses to wriggle out of a task. Reasons for procrastinating may align with one of the personas listed in Chapter One. (The Exceeder? The Casual Cavalier? The Smooth Operator? The Otherwise Occupied? The Analyst?) Procrastination can be caused by of-the-moment concerns, attitudes toward the task, or any number of academic, social, or emotional triggers.

However, it is possible for parents to work thoughtfully with their child to develop a go-to routine or strategic plan with options that will spark enthusiasm and reinforce perseverance. Stoking children's creativity and curiosity is a sure-fire way to kindle enthusiasm for a task, but it can be challenging to inspire unmotivated kids. Often it is helpful to transfer motivation from one area to another, starting with something that really interests them (such as sports, or music, or fashion), and then connecting it with the task (such as writing or math). For example, if a child is into sports but avoids math, he may beome motivated by an emphasis on statistics, like batting averages or team standings.

The end goal is to encourage kids to become intrinsically motivated. *Intrinsic motivation* comes from within; e.g., "I have to study French because I want to go to France as an exchange student some day, and I'll need to be able to speak the language." Some kids are motivated for the sake of learning or because they want to be able to apply knowledge.

On the other hand, *extrinsic motivation* refers to something external; e.g., "If I study French and do well, I'll get my name on the Honor Roll." For young children, extrinsic motivators might be rewards such as treats, high-fives, or gold stars. For older kids, parents might consider incorporating interests, hands-on learning opportunities, or targeted assistance. Of course, what we want in the long run is for children to do things more for the intrinsic motivation than for external rewards or recognition. However, extrinsic motivation can be a good place to begin and it can, in turn, lead to intrinsic motivation.[81]

Motivation, in all its forms, is important because it takes kids from one level to the next as they build upon their experiences and accomplishments. Children who do well in school and elsewhere are often motivated to continue to do well, to tackle difficult tasks, and to rebound when they confront stumbling blocks later on. Children who avoid tasks or activities can benefit from motivators that are well suited to the circumstances. (See Chapter 11 for a fuller discussion on motivation.)

When you talk with teachers, listen carefully to what they say about your child's motivation profile, learning experiences, and level of productivity (highs and lows, areas of stength and weakness, etc.). Thank teachers for their efforts. Too few parents do that, and teachers put forth more effort than most parents realize. Take the opportunity to listen carefully to concerns teachers may have about your child, and calmly share yours. You might want to ask a few questions about the classroom learning environment and how the teacher assigns work. Are due dates set in consultation with students and other teachers? How does the teacher monitor student progress? What does she think about the idea of setting small interim goals? What are the consequences for inaction? For example, what is the penalty for missing assignments versus late—and very late—assignments? What are the short-, medium-, and long-term implications if your child's work is left incomplete? Is the assigned work easy enough to do with effort, but not so difficult as to be off-putting?

Connect regularly with teachers, letting them know that although you may be inquisitive, you do not mean to be intrusive or judgmental, and that they can depend on you to be helpful, not overbearing.

Children can be taught to recognize when they feel tempted to procrastinate, and they can create an honesty plan to keep themselves on track. The old adage *Honesty is the best policy* can be a good motivator. Kids can ask themselves basic questions, such as: Is the task really that awful? How long do I think it will it take to complete? Is there some way to do it in small steps? Where can I get help if I need it? By asking themselves targeted questions like this and responding honestly—because they do not have to answer to anyone but themselves—kids can get a feel for a task and whether it is actually as demanding as it might seem. They also learn to develop accountability for their actions. (See Chapter 11 for more information about thinking processes.)

At Carlton University in Ottawa, Canada, there is a procrastination research group (www.procrastination.ca), and on the website are comics, poems, blogs, podcasts, and more, including lots of suggestions for procrastinators, many of which are applicable to kids.[82] Some notable ideas include developing a greater awareness of any intention to delay, so as to be able to address it when it occurs; identifying the costs of procrastinating; recognizing that tomorrow probably will not be that different from today (so might as well get started now); and learning not to overestimate the difficulty or unpleasantness of a task. Other themes have to do with learning to recognize common and hollow excuses; becoming more organized; investing less effort in multi-tasking and more in singular focus; and avoiding distractions, particularly by spending less time online. In fact, technology has acquired its own procrastination-related term—cyberslacking.

Although technology offers endless and exciting opportunities for learning and connectivity, the Internet can be a huge distraction for kids, causing them to procrastinate or preclude other tasks and activities. Parents can help kids avoid procrastination due to technological diversions by limiting computer time, or scheduling it for after tasks have been accomplished, or even blocking certain sites that take kids off course.

Of course, you do not want kids sitting online for extended periods of time (nor should you be doing that endlessly or they are liable to point fingers right back at you), but they can find useful ideas for overcoming procrastination at this Ottawa-based procrastination site. Kids are capable and can try out these ideas and strategies, one at a time. There are lots of *to-do* items on this list, which is rather ironic given that the issue at hand is a tendency *not* to do. However, with parents' assistance and encouragement, procrastination can be a thing of the past, and not the future.

Figure 6.2. Average to Bright Learners: More on Managing Procrastination

○ **Make it meaningful.** "Busy work" gets sidelined. If kids think something is going to be a waste of time or has too many repetitions—like multiplication questions or peeling potatoes—they will try to avoid doing it. However, if a task is relevant (or fun or exciting), they are more likely to get involved.

○ **Clarify.** If need be, clarify instructions, expectations, and available resources.

○ **Don't push the rush button.** Allow children the opportunity to think, consolidate ideas, and build upon what they already know.

○ **Show the way.** Demonstrate timeliness, preparation, organizational skills, and perseverance.[83]

○ **Praise conscientious behavior.** Let kids know you are proud of them, and why.

○ **Forgive faltering.** Try to understand the underlying reason for it. Kids learn from their setbacks, so provide helpful feedback.

○ **Foster autonomy.** Some children require more guidance than others as they work through a given task. The goal is to help them work toward academic independence, knowing that there are likely to be false starts, pauses, and hiccups along the way.

○ **Be fair.** Reasonable rules, structure, and timelines help set the tone for productivity.

○ **Worst first.** Suggest trying the most challenging or unappealing aspect of a task first. Once that is out of the way, the remainder is likely to seem less daunting or distasteful.

○ **Best, then the rest.** Alternatively, trying the easiest aspects of a task and mastering the basics first can sometimes give a feeling of accomplishment and spur momentum.

○ **Monitor progress.** Keep a steady eye on children's work. Consistency is better than intermittent attention to their progress.

Gifted Learners – Smart Beginnings

Gifted learners are those with exceptional capability such that they require specific kinds of learning opportunities to match their abilities at particular times and in particular areas.[84] Since a child may have gifted-level abilities in one or more of various academic subjects, the arts, leadership, or athletics, the pathways to exceptional achievement are complex and diverse.

Even extremely capable people sometimes choose to procrastinate, often to the dismay of others. Procrastination may sometimes even be in their areas of strength, as they say to themselves, "This is boring. I already know it." And other times they may procrastinate in their areas of weakness, as in, "This is complicated. I'll do it some other time." How ability translates into performance in any one area will differ from person to person, but generally speaking, even a very gifted learner cannot rest on her laurels. She must decide to apply her intelligence and abilities; she has to use what she has *conscientiously* in order to develop it further.

Action, not procrastination, is necessary to develop abilities. Author Malcolm Gladwell, in his acclaimed book *Outliers*, pointed out, "Achievement is talent plus preparation. The problem with this view is that the closer psychologists look at the careers of the gifted, the smaller the role innate talent seems to play and the bigger role preparation seems to play."[85]

Preparation demands action, not avoidance. Intellectually advanced students may believe they have a greater capacity to perform well at the 11th hour, especially if this has worked for them in the past. Once this last-minute approach becomes a tried and true technique, it becomes a hard habit to break. Some kids are content with this. They are unfazed by pressure situations and, in fact, work best when the clock is ticking down to the wire. (Remember the Pressure Pot persona?) If students do reasonably well this way, then parents may have to be accepting and come to terms with it—at least for the present. When this approach becomes problematic—that is, if it compromises a child's well-being, including health, academics, or family dynamics—then it is probably time to have a heart-to-heart talk about the implications, as well as more sensible ways to tackle task completion.

Recently, a boy named Joey was tested for giftedness and high-level ability at the age of eight, and the psychologist said she was going to give him a timed segment of the test. Many kids would have felt pressured, but Joey was totally at ease. He had no interest in the timer or in pushing himself. In fact, he paused for some water and to take a short break during the session. He did not complete the segment, but he did well. The tester indicated in her assessment report that Joey could have done better on this portion of the test but chose not to. He did not care about gifted identification or educational placement. As far as he was concerned, it was his decision to pace himself and complete the test however he saw fit. There are some situations that parents can only wonder at after the fact.

For those parents who scratch their heads because their talented and highly capable child is not inclined to answer questions, attend to his music, or focus on the art project they know he can do so beautifully—be patient. Sometimes kids wait for inspiration as an excuse (like adults often do!), but will get to things when they are ready. Readiness can be a big factor in getting things accomplished. It may help to consider this quote by Henry Ford: "Before anything else, getting ready is the secret of success."

Even the smartest, most academically advanced kids may have a hard time identifying what makes them ready, enthused, and efficient, or conversely, what makes them procrastinate. If a task is not compelling, they may not care that they are avoiding it because they have better things to think about. It is often easier for children—and adults, too—to make excuses and procrastinate than it is to think about why a task is unpleasant, insignificant, boring, or a waste of time.

As a result, there may be consequences to pay, and these can provide valuable lessons. For example, when kids find their future options (from band membership to course selections to college applications) short-circuited by their nonchalance, it may be time for some serious discussion (albeit not a lecture or a showdown) about their ideas around task completion.

It is also helpful for parents to find out about their child's specific learning needs—what they are and whether they are being addressed—on a subject-by-subject basis. What educational programs and services are available for gifted learners in your district? What kinds of learning opportunities are provided in your child's school? Are there other opportunities beyond school? Options might include congregated gifted classes, part-time programs, mentorships, project-based learning, extra-curricular activities and summer camps, leadership possibilities, and acceleration. A student is less likely to procrastinate and more likely to be responsive if she is content with her educational program and daily routine. The best learning environment is one where challenges are appropriate and expectations are well-defined and affirming, an environment that will both inspire thought and promote mastery. As Ralph Waldo Emerson observed, "Unless you try to do something beyond what you have already mastered, you will never grow."[86]

If a child enters a more demanding program, such as a full-time gifted or enrichment class or advanced-level studies, she will likely face new and possibly tough academic challenges. Parents can help their child decide whether to switch into such a program if the opportunity presents itself. Here are some questions to help guage her readiness. Does the program match her academic strengths? Is it consistent with her interests and her willingness to put forth effort? Does she realize the extent to which the learning environment may be more competitive? Is she okay knowing that she may have to work very hard to keep up with others in the class, and that excelling may be harder still? Parents can talk about what is involved. This includes sustained study, stretching the intellect, and learning from others. Even an extremely advanced child will not always be at the top of the class in the more demanding educational setting.

Kids who are extremely bright often gauge their own capabilities by using others who are not so advanced as their frame of reference. When a child moves into a milieu where *everyone* is advanced, that frame of reference shifts, and there is potentially more peer pressure.

Feelings of self-doubt may crop up, along with a tendency to procrastinate and lose focus, all of which can threaten the self-concept. Situations like this are sometimes referred to as the big fish, little pond effect.[87] The child may feel like a big fish in the less challenging classroom, but upon moving to a more advanced classroom, she feels that she doesn't stand out as much when compared to the others. Parents can reassure their child that she and her unique profile of abilities are what really matter; personal growth is most important, not comparisons to other students. Personal growth develops over time, with effort and resilience. Some kids eventually come to see themselves as "specialists" in their area of strength, and this helps them find their place in the new group. Parents can explain that challenges, difficulties, and mistakes are a very normal part of learning—even among gifted learners—and each fish, regardless of size or strengths, ultimately has to find its own way to stay afloat.

As kids explore larger pools and deeper knowledge, parents can assist their children by advocating for better programs and learning opportunities. Advocacy is an emotion-laden and time-consuming endeavor that can take a great deal of effort. There are strategies that work well, and common pitfalls that slow down the process.[88]

As a starting point for further thinking across all learner-ability levels, here are five practical tips for intelligent, effective advocacy.

Five Tips for Effective Advocacy

1. *Determine what is needed.* Figure out what specific needs you want met. Prioritize, and then be realistic about what can be changed.

2. *Gather information.* Pay attention to material that is relevant, based on what you hope to resolve. For example, it may be homework policies, challenge levels, or other concerns.

3. *Consider multiple points of view.* This includes those of teachers, administrators, consultants, and, of course, your child. Their perspectives and agendas might not align with yours. Listen carefully to what other people have to say. Be patient. Take notes during discussions and find out if there are any school-based records that you should know about.

4. *Collaborate.* Develop a step-by-step action plan with a reasonable timeline and workable parameters for everyone involved. Maintaining good relationships can be more important than getting what you want right away. A good relationship sets the stage for further work together and for change initiatives, and it opens doors with future teachers. People would much rather work with collaborators than dictators.

5. *Teach children to be respectfully assertive, discerning, and fairminded.* Help them recognize their individual learning needs. Talk with them about how they can advocate for themselves and how their own attitudes and behavior can contribute to their problems—or advancement—at school. Children have the power to use their voices, interests, strengths, attitudes, and resolve as springboards that can lead to exciting learning and accomplishments.[89]

It can be a motivating and worthwhile learning experience for children to see their parents advocating on their behalf and investing time and effort to ensure the best possible educational opportunities. When classroom work and homework demands are appropriately challenging and suited to their needs, kids are more inclined to show interest and grit, and to see things through. Children who become actively engaged in developing their own intelligence also become better prepared to set and reach their learning objectives, now as well as later.

Figure 6.3. Gifted Learners: Additional Ways to Manage Procrastination

○ **Become informed.** There are many excellent resources and parent organziations that offer information about gifted-related issues.[90]

○ **Set high but fair and realistic expectations.** Discuss them and tweak as necessary. Gifted learners actually appreciate appropriately high standards.

○ **Don't underestimate the importance of family and community.** When making decisions about schooling, everyone should work collaboratively to co-create and advocate for solutions that will benefit the child.

○ **Keep up to date.** Know what is happening with the child's special education program or individual education plan.

○ **Remember that gifted learners are not likely to excel in everything.** Encourage kids to work hard and be dynamic in all they can do and to be persistent when confronting inevitable blips on the radar screen.

○ **There are many different ways of being gifted.** It is more about *doing* than *being*. There is no one sure-fire way of nurturing giftedness that will work for every child.

○ **Be sensitive to the ever-changing nature of kids' temperaments and the pressures of their daily lives.** They are striving to meet various demands set by parents, teachers, others, and, ultimately, themselves—and no matter how smart they might be, they are still growing and learning how to prioritize, juggle responsibilities, and be successful.

CHAPTER 7

Procrastination and Perfectionism

"Even if you're on the right track, you'll get run over if you just sit there."

~ Will Rogers

Procrastination and perfectionism are often linked together. A perfectionist insists on absolutely top-notch results; therefore, you would think a perfectionist would value task completion and be unlikely to procrastinate. After all, how can someone hope to achieve perfection in a task without actually taking the steps required to reach its conclusion? However, many perfectionists do procrastinate, and many procrastinators have perfectionist tendencies. To understand this, we begin by looking at expectations—one's own, as well as those set by others—and the thoughts and actions that follow.

Expectations

A child who thinks her work must be perfect in order to be acceptable often becomes worried and stressed. She may think, "What if I make mistakes? What if other people think I'm stupid or weak?" She may conclude that it is better to put something off than to do it poorly. Keep in mind that for a perfectionist, *poor* work in their eyes may still be just shy of outstanding.

By procrastinating, a person can rationalize that if only she had given herself more time, the outcome might have been perfect. By making excuses or avoiding a task, she may think she is more in control of her actions and the demands she has set for herself. She also prevents those close to her—parents, teachers, or peers—from judging her as inept.

While a child's perfectionistic tendencies may be an underlying cause of procrastination, lofty expectations from parents and teachers can also add to the problem. For instance, when Warren was in grade 10, he put all of his effort into a book report. He received a grade of 70%—right at the class average, but he did not want to tell his parents about this because they were always talking about how his sister made the Honor Roll. They had just recently said to him, "Wouldn't it be nice if you were at the top of your class, too?" Then, to make matters worse, his English teacher wrote several critical comments across his paper in bright red ink. She did not say one thing about the positive or creative aspects of his report. Warren's "all or nothing" type of thinking led him to conclude that his teacher did not like his work—"What's the point in even trying? I'll never get an A from her." He was thwarted by the exceedingly high expectations being placed upon him by others.

Warren's next major assignment was to write an analysis of the cultural issues influencing the main character in the novel the class was studying. He procrastinated, partly due to his experience with the book report the previous week, and also because of his self-imposed perfectionistic pressure to perform at his best. Warren decided he would write the paper the day before it was due. However, since he was rushed, he did not have time to research it properly, and he ended up not handing anything in. As a result, he became even more discouraged and angry with himself; he thought he had let everyone down. The high expectations set by Warren's parents and teachers were eroding his self-confidence.

I had an experience somewhat similar to Warren's. In third grade, I received 99% in spelling on my final report card, but when I took it home, my mother asked, "Why didn't you get 100%?" I still recall the disappointment in her voice as she asked this short but stinging question. The answer was that I had lost the one percent because of a three-letter word! I had written *it's* instead of *its* when the teacher dictated a sentence during a spelling test. Although I am an author now and quite disciplined, I am still admittedly quick to berate myself when I make a careless spelling error.

Parents should ask themselves whether their expectations are a factor in their child's procrastination. Is he putting things off because he thinks he is not good enough? Is he postponing potential criticism and evaluation by you? Consider your role in the life of the young person you are concerned about and take a few moments to examine your expectations. Are they overwhelming or are they realistic based on your child's areas of strength and weakness? What about your behavior or body language? What messages do they convey? You may want to strike up an exploratory conversation to uncover how your child perceives your expectations about things like schoolwork, chores, commitments, and so on—and also how you feel about the expectations you set. Discovering misunderstandings and simply indicating a willingness to listen might help your child overcome his procrastination and perfectionist tendencies.

And when it comes to school-based expectations, be savvy. As a parent, you are entitled to feel comfortable and supported at your child's school. Ask questions if you want to know more about subject-specific program expectations, or to find out if programming meets your child's educational needs. Keep your eyes open for indicators that *flexibility* and *fit* are guiding principles in use—that is, that there is respect for individuality and adaptability in the approaches employed in the classroom.

Figure 7.1. Expectations: How to Find Healthier Perspectives and Circumvent Procrastination

○ **Write it down.** Have children write down expectations you both agree to, in language that is easily understood. Keep this handy. Index cards or tech devices can be useful to record the necessary information.

○ **Pause periodically.** Encourage kids to pause occasionally to re-evaluate what they are doing and see if they are staying on course with what is expected of them. If they are veering off track, they may have to make adjustments. Stopping now and then to evaluate is a strategy that will serve them well in all kinds of future situations.

- ○ **Who says the beaten path is the best way to go?** Entertain creative approaches, invite longer incubation times (for percolating thoughts and brainstorming), and possibly create brand new expectations as things evolve. Be gracious about revising expectations and offer to help with this as needed.

- ○ **Don't expect siblings or grade peers to be in lockstep.** Adjust expectations so they are suited to the individual. Don't compare people or accomplishments.

- ○ **Find and share stories about famous and not-so-famous people.** In particular, focus on individuals who met and exceeded expectations in various fields, including those of particular interest to the child.

- ○ **Avoid superficiality.** Ensure that the learning or the task is meaningful—that is, worth starting and then striving to complete.

Feelings: Being Overwhelmed or Concerned

A perfectionist may well realize that she is not likely to attain perfection. How does this feel? It can be overwhelmingly disappointing, or embarrassing, or stressful. Procrastination offers an easy solution, a way to postpone or retreat from concerns about having to achieve to perfection. And if the person manages to perform exceptionally well in spite of procrastinating, she can feel even more pleased with herself. This enhances her sense of self-worth; she feels smart and capable; and she once again is primed to strive for perfection. So the cycle continues.

The search for perfection can be relentless. Miss Gilroy, the math teacher, does not understand why Francesca cried when she got an A on her mid-term test. Isn't that a terrific mark? For most people—but for Francesca, only an A+ would do. Whenever she cannot solve a math problem, Francesca becomes physically distraught; her stomach aches and she starts to feel queasy. In her attempts to be perfect, she pushes herself night after night, studying diligently. People like Francesca who strive for perfection can easily feel overwhelmed by demands—becoming upset, self-critical, and even disenchanted with learning. These kinds of feelings can lead to different behaviors, including procrastination.[91]

You may be able to help your perfectionist child understand that the pursuit of excellence can be rewarding as long as learning agendas are healthy and not carried to the extreme.[92] Inability to reach perfection does not have to be a threat to self-esteem. Ask your child to think carefully about what she can and cannot accomplish within a given time frame and context. Talk with her about the concept of "good enough"—that is, to appreciate something that is acceptable and done well (and without causing sleeplessness or distress) in the given time allowed. Encourage her to ask for assistance when needed. There's no shame in that! Teach her how to defer judgment and how to focus on the effort and progress—the journey—instead of the end point. Kids can be guided so they see tasks as interesting challenges, as opposed to trials or hard-won products wide open for criticism, and parents can provide examples of this in their own lives.

Parents can show how to feel satisfied about setting and meeting realistic standards rather than seeking "perfect" outcomes. They can discuss why perfection is not generally a realistic end goal. When people wake up in the morning and say to themselves, "I will do perfectly in all respects today," they are only setting themselves up for failure. Instead, a person can emphasize the value of being comfortably productive. This kind of reassurance will help children forge ahead and accept their limitations as well as their strengths. They will be less likely to procrastinate, even when difficulties seem insurmountable, and they will enjoy a healthier orientation to learning.

There is some controversy about the actual extent to which perfectionism may be a cause or contributing factor for procrastination, and causal connections between the two are inconsistent when looking at groups.[93] Nevertheless there *are* correlations between perfectionists who choose to delay action for various reasons and procrastinators who put things off but strive toward perfection.[94]

Here are some more tips in Figure 7.2 for parents of children who procrastinate and exhibit perfectionism.

Figure 7.2. Feelings: How to Handle the Emotions Surrounding Procrastination

○ **Use criticism judiciously and constructively.** Comment on the behavior, not the child. You are coaching the child to the next level, not just finding fault.

○ **Help children understand that they don't have to excel all the time.** They should not equate self-worth with achievement. It can be troubling when your self-worth rests only on whether you achieve perfection. Be careful how often you say, "Just do your best." Perfectionists will take you at your word.

○ **Have children purposely make a small mistake.** In other words, have them *court* imperfection. What happens? It's not the end of the world and civilization does continue. For example, a child who puts the blocks in the crayon bin and vice versa will still be able to find and play with them the next day. A student who hands in a paper with margins that are not quite formatted properly will likely find that the content matters more than the alignment.

○ **Share the load.** Encourage children to work constructively with others instead of independently so as to share responsibilities. This can help reduce pressure and also show that different people have different work styles and approaches.

○ **Employ humor.** People sometimes joke about procrastination, and it can help to take the edge off, e.g., "Someday is not a day of the week." It is certainly better than feeling pent-up guilt, discomfort, or even anxiety due to putting things off.

○ **Help children differentiate between perfection and success.** They are not the same. Try teaching self-guided imagery whereby children envision quality or excellence as opposed to perfection. For instance, picturing a term paper with many thoughtful or creative answers can elicit feelings of satisfaction even if the work is not error free. Thinking about sticking a balance beam dismount in gymnastics after recovering from the wobbles helps focus on a successful event.

○ **Examine the lives of eminent people.** Talk about their journeys, obstacles, setbacks, resiliency, and how they managed to keep going. What strategies worked for them that might be useful?

○ **Accept assistance from others.** Show children how to get help—and why it's okay. Be available to help or to suggest someone who can. Provide a way for them to ask for help and save face. Give them three pieces of paper—green for "I'm doing fine," yellow for "I could use some help, but I can keep going for now," and red for "I'm really stuck"—and tell them to let you know how well they are doing and when they need assistance by placing one on their worktop for you to see when you are nearby.

○ **Priorities are learning and experience, not performance or product.** Help children understand the distinction. Encourage some spontaneity and flexibility.

○ **Less rigidity is not only acceptable, it's desirable.** Reinforce the concept that *high but realistic* standards are admirable. Structure is good, but too much of anything can be stifling and off-putting. Everything in moderation—including moderation.

○ **Have fun!** Provide opportunities for children to participate in various activities and hobbies that are fun and not timed or competitive in nature.

Sometimes children need guidance to be able to relax and redirect their focus. The ideal is for them to experience the fullness of learning—a lifelong journey composed of accomplishment and joy, but not perfection.

Positivity

There are two very different but connected aspects about doing things exceedingly well. The first aspect has to do with *children's* attitudes—and cultivating an accepting outlook toward activities. The second aspect has to do with *parents'* attitudes—and cultivating an accepting outlook toward procrastination. Positive attitudes do not just happen. They require nurturing.

You may be familiar with the song *High Hopes*, made famous by Frank Sinatra. Here are some of the lyrics:

Just what makes that little old ant
Think he'll move that rubber tree plant?
Anyone knows an ant, can't
Move a rubber tree plant.

But he's got high hopes, he's got high hopes,
He's got high apple pie in the sky hopes.
So any time you're gettin' low,
'stead of lettin' go,
Just remember that ant.
Oops! There goes another rubber tree plant![95]

Sometimes, an upbeat attitude and the willingness to try is exactly what is needed to make the seemingly impossible seem possible after all. Children who are prone to dawdle or delay may need help acquiring a more confident and resolute outlook toward whatever it is they are avoiding. Ask them what they are thinking. Is it too difficult? Then have them try and make it easier by seeing what they *can do*. Is it too big? Tackle it in smaller chunks. Is it too easy? Think of a way to extend the idea and make it more challenging. Is it too boring? Look for relevance by connecting it to something that interests them. In other words, whatever the issue, there is usually a positive perspective that can turn things around.

Positive psychology is the study of the virtues and strengths that underlie the ability to be resilient and thrive. It is based on the premise that people seek to lead meaningful lives, enrich their experiences, and nurture what is best within themselves. For those who want to find out more about positive psychology, a good place to start is www. positivepsychology.org.

Positivity is not a superhuman power but a real and doable one. Having faith in one's abilities is something that applies not only to Olympian athletes or advanced learners, but to everyone. Positivity is an energy force that can be nurtured anywhere. It means being upbeat and constructive, not only seeing the upside but actively possessing, demonstrating, and encouraging a growth mindset. An important aspect of positivity involves striving to nurture it on daily basis. It is not just about adopting a "sunny outlook." Rather it is about routinely paying close attention to those things in life that give you pleasure. It might be music, people who make you laugh, or regularly scheduled conversations that will make you happy, and these experiences and triggers can be incorporated into your routine and environment and become a part of daily life. Quite simply, happiness—and taking note of what generates it—is motivating.[96]

The practice of mindfulness is increasingly capturing the interest of educators, especially as a way to strengthen student-teacher connectivity, but it has other applications as well. Mindfulness is the process of paying close attention to what is happening in a single moment. Not being judgmental, just being as fully aware as possible by attuning to words, actions, senses, breathing, and more. Learning to respond to and connect directly with the world around us can enhance relationships, experiences, communication, and resilience. Exercises that promote mindfulness serve to stimulate self-awareness, self-regulation, and personal well-being.[97] Mindfulness can enrich the lives of parents and children and increase their vitality.

Sheer will and grit are also motivating and help propel people forward. Parents can point to this, but they can also show how their own positive outlooks invigorate them and make them feel enthusiastic—how they focus on pleasure rather than perfection, and how this leads to better productivity. Parents can demonstrate just how they get down to the business of doing things they find onerous. It might be cleaning the basement by doing one section each day to music, or starting tax forms long before they are due in order to spend only an hour a day on them, or scraping a thick layer of ice off the car windshield and having hot cocoa as a reward. How do you make a task more appealing? What is necessary in order to take that first step?

Researcher Timothy Pychyl, who studied the connections between procrastination and mood, found that regulating emotions can be a key to overcoming procrastination.[98] Recognizing discomfort about performing a particular chore or task and then rising above it can bolster your mood. Instead of feeling annoyed or guilty about procrastinating, children can learn to replace negative thoughts with positive ones. That, in turn, will increase their willpower. Pychyl recommends a strategy he calls *time travel*—something kids will likely enjoy. In this exercise, a child "projects herself" into the future just by using her imagination where she can imagine the good feelings she will have upon completing a task, or the bad feelings she will have if she does not complete it. This sort of exercise enables kids to anticipate the impact of procrastination on their emotions. Positive emotions energize and spur action. And bad feelings can transform to good ones once a project is started or a deadline is met.

Another mood-repair strategy involves self-forgiveness.[99] When a child blames herself for procrastinating, or has negative thoughts about it, or feels she cannot live up to perfection, this can further block her productivity. These children need help learning to forgive themselves—to get rid of feelings such as shame or dismay—and they may need encouragement to go beyond self-reproach in order to get started on a task. Even small first steps can launch momentum. Infusing hope and forgiveness, too, can boost a person's mood.

How can parents adopt a positive outlook when they are feeling frustrated, annoyed, or worried about their child? It is hard to smile when you are unsure or you feel like scolding, shouting, or giving up. But a positive attitude can make all the difference between determination and defeat. We all make choices in life, and how we value our choices and the outcomes rests on attitude.[100]

The ABCDE model of disputing or managing negative thoughts provides an interesting course of action for parents and children to consider.[101] Developed by psychologist Martin Seligman and his colleagues, it is a systematic process of self-talk for understanding and managing stressful situations. It can be used as a template for helping kids become more positive when facing difficulties. Here's how it works:

A is for *activating*—identify and focus on the event: "I have trouble getting my math work in by the due date."

B is for *beliefs*—become aware what your thoughts are about it: "I never seem to have enough time."

C is for *consequences*—decide how you feel about your beliefs and what may realistically happen: "I'm unhappy and pressured because my grades will suffer."

D is for *dispute*—challenge the negative thought from B and replace it with something more positive: "I can make an effort and get a routine in place. I can set aside some time to work on math every evening after supper."

E is for *effect*—think about how you feel after taking a more positive stance: "I'm relieved. I have a plan now."

The ABCDE plan is efficient because it starts with the individual identifying the gist of a problem, and then recognizing thoughts and feelings about it. Then the person moves deliberately from negativity to positivity with feelings of gratification and accomplishment as a result. Some steps may be more difficult, but parents can help kids talk their way from A to E by considering one point at a time, and taking a break if necessary.

Consider these additional ideas in Figure 7.3 to harness positivity for yourself and your kids.

Figure 7.3. Tips for Finding Positivity

○ **There's an old axiom:** *Better late than never.* Convey confidence in the child's ability to succeed, even if not as promptly as anticipated.

○ **Validate.** Children may have legitimate reasons for procrastinating. See Chapter 1 for examples. Sometimes leniency can promote positivity.

○ **Aim for flexible timelines.** Flexibility can be accommodating of children's needs. Show them how to rework a timeline if a goal is not met.

○ **Seek out positive frames of reference and attainable goals.**
See Chapter 10 for more on goal-setting.

○ **Use time wisely.** Help children appreciate that there are
limited hours in a day, so they have to think carefully about
how to use them wisely. For long-term projects, have them
start by listing their steps and estimating how long each one
will take. As the early steps are completed, check to see how
much time they actually take, and then rework the timeline
to allow for new estimates.

○ **Create a positive environment.** Infuse the working space with
happiness-boosters such as photos, music, posters, lighting,
potpourri, art, or whatever is personally inspiring.

○ **Share the vibe.** Okay, so procrastination may not be the most
admirable trait, yet many people procrastinate. Have a look at
this short and snappy YouTube video (*Procrastination—The
Musical*) created by a group of teenagers and posted at http://
youtu.be/Xi3aEGo8y-E. Feel the vibe, have a chuckle, and
then get ready to tackle procrastination anew.[102]

○ **Aim for manageable goals.** If a goal is specific and looks
doable, there is less likelihood of disenchantment and, ultimately, disappointment. (A little ant aspiring to move a rubber
tree plant is not the best example of "doable," but there is
something to be said for gumption. Think: *Where there is a
will, there is a way.*)

○ **Find a healthy outlet for negative emotions.** Try breathing
deeply and counting slowly to 10, thinking of a pleasant
experience, or engaging in physical activity. Share techniques
for getting rid of negativity, thinking more constructively, or
acquiring a measured and peaceful outlook.

CHAPTER 8

Can and Able—Or Not?

*"There are risks and costs to action. But they are far less than
the long range risks of comfortable inaction."*

~ John F. Kennedy

Few individuals are accomplished in all things. However, people who welcome and thrive on challenge and who seek to expand their skills and range of knowledge generally feel pleased about their accomplishments. They also realize that by putting forth effort they gain control of their skills and competencies.

However, even people who can do things easily may procrastinate for various reasons. Think back to Katrina from Miss Gilroy's class in Chapter 1. Katrina is bored stiff during math lessons. She would rather do anything than the assigned work—which is too easy—so she puts it off. At the other end of the spectrum, there are children who are less proficient, or who lack certain skills, who may decide to procrastinate rather than tackle something that seems difficult.

This chapter is about potential, preferences, and issues children face as they experience change or take risks. Each of these three topics has a connection with procrastination and accomplishment. First, take a moment to think of people who are really accomplished at something. Now think of what they may not do nearly as well. Highly proficient science students, talented artists, skilled athletes—each of these individuals may have one or more area of expertise, and yet may be more or less average in other areas. And that's okay. Sidney Crosby is an outstanding hockey player.[103] He does not have to be great at writing sonnets. Nelson Mandela was an inspirational politician and humanitarian. He was not a biochemist. Taylor Swift and Jennifer Hudson are talented young women who have won numerous music awards. But can either of them fly an airplane? There may be no constraints on what people can and cannot do, but there is inevitably an extent to how well they may be able to do it; no one can be expected to excel at everything.

Accomplishment—such as meeting educational goals, reaching beyond one's comfort zone to tackle a challenge, helping a friend, or finishing a practice session in sports or music—makes a child feel good about himself and enables him to progress in new and self-fulfilling ways.[104] It is akin to developing one's potential, though that word elicits some controversy.

Potential

Sometimes people refer to a child's potential as though it is something that is known and predictable. We may hear a parent or teacher say, "Luanne's not working up to her potential in history class," or "Paige has a lot of potential, but she needs to work harder." However, potential is really an invisible unknown that cannot be measured. Assessing a child's ability at any one point in time provides very few clues about her potential for success in the future. Too many factors and influences in life can affect a person's later success.

When a child procrastinates, adults sometimes heave a fretful sigh and exclaim, "She's not living up to her potential." What they are really saying is that the child is not living up to *their* expectations or standards. Rather than focusing on anyone's potential as an end goal—after all, potential is elusive and not clear cut—it is far more productive to encourage her to develop a strong work ethic based on her own choices and aspirations.[105] You also can encourage her to come closer to meeting whatever bar has been set—assuming it is fair and realistic. Part of the job of being a good parent or teacher involves encouraging children to try new things and to get better at the things they can already do.

Most of us think about procrastination in terms of speed. So if someone does not do a task quickly, we feel as if they are procrastinating. But advanced learners are not necessarily fast thinkers, nor do they always learn quickly.

Sometimes kids have trouble identifying or expressing what is causing them to delay. There may be issues under the surface that they cannot explain but that influence their behavior. People are not always consciously aware of why they act or feel a certain way—for example, why they are afraid, uncomfortable, or lack confidence. Sometimes past experiences, memories, expectations, or arguments can trigger an aversion or avoidance behavior. Or they may not have a vocabulary of emotions to be able to put their finger on just what the issue is. The ability is there, but inaction suggests otherwise.

We cannot tell which child will accomplish great things in life, or who will flounder, lead, or inspire. And although schooling is essential, it alone does not define who or what a child will become or what her potential might be. We must simply motivate kids to try hard in whatever they choose to do. Bill Gates is an entrepreneurial and philanthropic trailblazer, and he sums it up well: "The more you learn, the more you have a framework that the knowledge fits into."[106] That learning can fuel accomplishment, regardless of preconceived potential.

Figure 8.1. Potential: How to Find Healthier Perspectives to Fight Procrastination

○ **Don't make assumptions about anyone's potential.** No one knows what the future holds. Focus on children's efforts or on what they are doing well *now*, regardless of past performance.

○ **Ensure that what is being asked of a child is something within his range of capability.** The task should be something he can accomplish with some comfortable stretching.[107]

○ **Model time for reflection.** Thinking about a task ahead of time helps a person figure out the angles and possible hurdles, and lessens the urge to procrastinate. Together, try color coding a list of what looks hard and easy, or what will take only a little or a great deal of time. The sorting process adds structure to children's thinking.

○ **Check out a planner.** Try the one on Deborah Ruf's Talent-igniter web page.[108] It is a tool designed to help track children's education programs and achievements in order to help kids make choices and broach tasks that are well suited to their abilities.

○ **Learn to be an effective advocate.** Help ensure that a child's schooling fits his needs, including ability levels, interests, and learning preferences. (See Chapter 6 for more on advocacy.)

Preferences

Everyone has things they really enjoy doing and things they would much rather avoid. Looking at the big picture, varied preferences are probably a good thing and make the world go around a bit more smoothly. After all, if we *all* focused on or avoided the same activities—such as math, reading, painting, playing soccer, or whatever—it would pose endless logistical problems as well as make for a pretty dull world.

Even infants have preferences. Maybe it is as simple as choosing the small toy giraffe instead of the colorful plastic rings, or mashed sweet potatoes rather than barley cereal. Toddlers may want to read a specific book over and over, or carry around a favorite stuffed animal all day long. As kids get older, there are more choices, more influences, and more decisions to make in order to manage their more complex lives. And consequences of the decision-making can become increasingly tangled, too, involving schooling, social relationships, personal values, career choice, and other aspects of life.

Parents often set the standard for what their children should or should not like, do, say, wear, eat, and so on. These standards may be seen by kids as realistic or geared too high or low. They may have to do with big issues (like health, education, or respect for others), or little ones (like television schedules or how to make the bed). Children also set standards for themselves that are often based on personal, and sometimes inexplicable, preferences.

We all think and behave in different ways, enjoying some things and steering clear of others. Wanting ice cream versus broccoli for example, is not a serious matter; however, decisions about proper eyeglasses, helmet use while skateboarding, or completing homework assignments are more important. Parents can explain why certain decisions leave little room for negotiation, especially when it has to do with a child's health or welfare, as is the case with eye care, head protection, or actually doing homework. Even so, we cannot truly know what is going on in someone else's mind as they choose what to do or how to follow through. As the saying goes, one person's pleasure is another's labor (or pain, annoyance, fear, obsession, or cause for delay). Children are no different.

Children may see things as exciting or boring—or maybe even a bit of both. One child loves the writing assignment about a trip to the zoo while another is excited about train stations. Each is bored by the other's essay topic.[109] Yet that essay about the trip to the zoo may include both intriguing bits (seeing how penguins change directions underwater in a flash) and dull ones (waiting behind the crowd of taller people until you can actually see the penguins). Sylvia Rimm, a psychologist who writes about underachievement, points out that not all children value the same tasks, regardless of whether value comes from efforts or from results. She emphasizes the importance of building value—of the task, the outcome, or both. This leads to motivation.[110]

The boy next door to me grew up playing the drums and the xylophone—at all hours, and sometimes with the windows open. For the past 12 years, I have marveled at his stamina—and his talent. His parents supported his choice of instruments and his passion to excel. He has won awards and recently accepted a scholarship to a prestigious music academy in Europe. What fuelled his achievement? His parents' encouragement and his own desire. He rarely procrastinated when it came to practicing because he valued music-making, enjoyed it, and took great pride in his accomplishments. It was, quite simply, what he wanted to do, and how he preferred to spend time and energy. When children sense that they have ownership of their activities and that their learning choices are respected, they are more inclined to commit to them and see them through.

Parents can assist children with their choices and with decision-making—not by deciding things for them but by showing them sensible steps for seeking options, weighing alternatives, and investing themselves in motivating activities, as well as how to arrive at satisfying outcomes and insightful resolutions. Talk together about why planning and decision making are important. Here are five steps to consider: 1) distinguish what is relevant from what is not; 2) think about what is involved in deciding one way or another; 3) look at the broader picture; 4) consider if and how various talents, strengths, and resources can be tapped; and 5) discuss the decision you have arrived at, including why or how it can be revisited over time and why it is important to start moving forward.

"Nothing is so fatiguing as the eternal hanging on of an uncompleted task," said William James, philosopher and psychologist. Regardless of whether it has to do with music, art, mathematics, language, thinking skills, or any other area of focus, parents can share their own experiences, showing that *doing* can be gratifying. *Doing* is also necessary before aspirations can become realities.

All children need encouragement to become doers—"They need to express themselves and have their thinking and talents supported."[111] Parents are well positioned to emphasize *can* and *will*, as opposed to *cannot* or *will not*.

Figure 8.2. Working with Preferences to Manage Procrastination

- ○ **Be accepting.** Honor children's preferences and encourage their interests. Don't try to control them or their choices.

- ○ **Avoid using negative language.** For example, think *tough*, not *impossible*; *could*, not *should*; *choose to do*, not *must do*.

- ○ **Don't set "forever rules."** Allow for some maneuverability. For example, "Absolutely no phone calls until all your homework is done" is inflexible. Sometimes kids prefer to consult with others and can benefit from some down time in the midst of their work.

- ○ **Be specific.** Whether it has to do with preferences or intentions, thinking in abstract terms or broad generalities can make it difficult to get down to business. Help children learn to devise a focused and workable plan. It should include mastery goals—"Learn 10 spelling words"—and not vague attainment goals—"Get an A on the zoo essay"—that depend on someone else's judgment.

○ **Help kids prepare for competitive experiences.** Over time, preferences and hard work may lead to high-level achievements (as happened with my neighbor), and kids may find themselves in competition with others for awards, scholarships, or program eligibility. Win/lose situations can be stressful. Some children may strive; others may balk. Parents can teach kids about good sportsmanship, perseverance, and resilience.[112] Measuring one's own growth, even in the face of a loss, can provide comfort.

Making Changes and Taking Risks

Doing may involve some measure of accommodating—to expectations and to things that happen. It may also involve risk-taking as a result of new or unforeseen circumstances. What kinds of changes do kids confront, and how might these affect their productivity and accomplishments?

Parents cannot possibly anticipate all the various changes that occur in a child's life. Change might be anticipated or unexpected, big or little, painstakingly slow or lightning fast. Many children experience a transition from one educational program to another. Others experience changes such as moving to a different town or country and leaving friends behind, acquiring a new sibling, or having to cope with family upheavals such as divorce, unemployment, or the death of a loved one. Change affects children in different ways. And changes made by choice are easier than changes that are imposed. Think about change and transitions that are in the offing within your child's world—along with potential implications.

Here are some basic guidelines and a few practical strategies for supporting change processes.[113] You can start by filling in the blank: "Change can be _____." You could be thinking along the lines of *scary, inevitable,* or *inspirational,* but there are countless possibilities. Descriptors will vary and will depend on the particular situation, the perceived impact of the change, and how the individual feels about previous change experiences. For instance, a school change that involves switching from public school to homeschooling, or moving to a new neighborhood and making new friends, or transferring to a class with a specialized curriculum, can be worrisome, pleasant, motivating—or no big deal.

Parents who recognize and appreciate the complexities of change and take time to reflect upon the potential implications set the tone for good development opportunities for their children. There's no doubt that we live in an ever-changing world. Successful change entails planning, preparation, and commitment—as well as adaptation. When children fail to adapt well to change, they tend to be less willing or even able to take on everyday responsibilities and tasks. They may procrastinate, putting things off until they feel more relaxed or confident or believe that things have stabilized. That being said, remember that "a ship is safe in harbor, but that's not what ships are for."[114] No one stands still forever. Stability can be elusive, and change is inevitable.

Parents can help kids adjust to change. One approach is to show them how to anticipate what lies ahead. Talk about how to chart a sensible course of action. Chat with children about the reasons for change and what will likely occur as a result, academically, emotionally, or socially. Let them know that you will be there to offer them support as needed. If you think a change is likely to be unsettling, discuss ways to make it happen smoothly, perhaps by adjusting the extent, pace, or nature of the change process. List things that will be easy to let go and those that are eagerly anticipated. Kids who are helped to feel at ease when confronting change of various types are better able to handle matters as they arise. They are also more inclined to take sensible risks, and these in turn might lead to more changes—some of which may culminate in new directions for personal growth.

For example, the status quo at your child's school may be shifting as children's individual needs are identified and addressed, as educational policies are revisited, or as teaching practices and programs are refined. There may be modifications, technological advances, innovative modes of instruction, or new learning environments. Some kids adapt to such changes seamlessly, whereas others resist, perhaps because they feel unsure or intimidated. Change represents the unknown, and it can be disruptive. Beginning a new program (say, a gifted class or an arts-based course of studies) can be a risky move and feelings can run high. But with preparation and guidance, most changes can be managed well.

It is okay for children to take thoughtful, sensible risks. Every new task involves some degree of risk of failure or being evaluated by others, or even being hurt, but that is how people grow and learn. When you first attempted to ride a bike or learned to skate, you may have avoided trying and you probably fell many times. In other words, there was risk involved and you learned to manage it.

Parents can talk with kids about different kinds of risks, using examples that are personally relevant. These might have to do with serious concerns, such as putting off drinking enough on a hot summer day; sidestepping school assignments and missing important deadlines; or remaining silent when witnessing a bullying incident. By teaching children about foolhardy versus safe risk-taking and giving them all the information they need, parents help them cope more effectively.

However, children's beliefs about their abilities—at school, at home, on a sports field, in an arts studio, or elsewhere—emerge from what they have been able (or unable) to do in the past. They need to learn to size up the risks and benefits in a situation, and to know their supports—what and whom they can rely upon when adjusting to changing circumstances or confronting something risky. Parents can help kids appreciate that because life is full of changes, we all have times when we lack confidence or question how (or if) to proceed. As children get older, they develop a better understanding of what they can do well, what they need to work really hard at, and when they have to make the best of a situation by finding a way to deal with it. Procrastination may be one possibility, though it certainly may not be the best because it may lead to more self-doubt and have a negative impact on well-being.

Here are six foundational thoughts for parents, with strategic tips for helping children develop adaptability, resilience, and forbearance in times of change or when things seem risky.

1. ***Knowledge**—is empowering.* Take careful stock of the change or risk and share the key information with your kids. Better yet, teach your kids how to acquire their own knowledge about possible risks that might be involved in something, as well as the potential benefits.

2. **Reflection**—*is a constructive process.* Think about the possible implications of the change or risk, particularly with respect to your child's comfort level. Take into account his feelings, reactions, and resilience in previous kinds of circumstances.

3. **Support systems**—*can lighten the load.* Knowing that one has others to rely on during times of change or risk can facilitate the process. Check out the support services at school and within the community, including people involved in planning and implementing any changes and others who might provide assistance.

4. **Complexities**—*can be simplified.* Can the situation be altered to be more accommodating of your child's individual needs? Do you foresee any adjustment problems that can be offset?

5. **The unexpected**—*is inevitable.* Unanticipated factors and outside influences can affect a change process or alter the riskiness of a task. Note these as they arise and encourage your child to do the same—deviations might offer new opportunities.

6. **Professional help**—*is available.* Seek professional advice if it becomes apparent that your child needs increased assistance or coping strategies; for example, if your child can't sleep, won't eat, loses interest in friends, or experiences some other unusual problem, this may indicate a need for help.

When children confront change or are on the brink of something new or potentially risky, parents can revisit some or all of these six reference points to help kids get over the hurdles and feel more capable. It may well be a matter of transition—from procrastination, to action, and in time, to triumph.

Figure 8.3. Changes and Risk-Taking: Dealing with Intimidation and Procrastination

○ **Put it into words.** Give kids ample opportunity to express their concerns or apprehensions. Verbalizing and sharing thoughts can help them get past a sense of isolation. Having someone else on board can be a calming influence and mitigate the risk.

○ **Pick your spot.** Choose a comfortable and quiet space for open dialogue. Move away from shaky ground in order to gain solid footing.

○ **Be honest.** Provide only as much detail as a child is able to handle. Children vary in their abilities to process information; their cognitive levels differ with age, past experiences, and personal development.

○ **Address issues one at a time.** Don't try to deal with everything all at once.

○ **Pay particular attention to behavior that is markedly out of step.** This might take the form of temper tantrums, crying spells, isolation, or other responses that interfere with daily functioning. Take time to discuss the behavioral concerns with the child to find out what is going on and to develop ways to improve the behavior.

○ **Hug.** When changes and risks seem daunting sometimes the best reassurance and comfort come in the form of a warm hug or a few quiet moments together.

○ **If a child feels like talking, listen.** If he doesn't feel like talking, don't push too hard. Just be available. Ask if there is a better time or place for a chat.

○ **Set an example.** Through words and deeds, emphasize and model safe risk-taking and adaptability in the face of change. This can instill confidence.[115]

CHAPTER 9

Children's Daily Avoidance

"In a moment of decision, the best thing you can do is the right thing to do. The worst thing you can do is nothing."
~ Theodore Roosevelt

Procrastination can be chronic or sporadic. Some children establish a pattern of not starting or completing decision-making, tasks, or activities. For others, putting things off may be an occasional occurrence when they encounter a dilemma or have what they feel is reasonable cause to procrastinate in a particular situation. Many reasons are listed in Chapter 1, but a frequent theme involves power struggles, and these often arise around issues of messiness, chores, and homework. There are lots of strategies to help kids overcome procrastination tendencies in these areas.

Our Hurried World

We live in a fast-paced world. Daily life sometimes gets in the way of our best intentions to forge ahead. People are expected to multi-task. Even small children can simultaneously eat, type a message on an electronic device, listen to music, and carry on a conversation. Drivers navigate the roads while talking or tapping on a cell phone, although it is dangerous and illegal in many places. In a society where many things happen all at once, we have to prioritize, make allowances and sometimes excuses—deciding what to do *now* and what to put off until *later*. It's almost a new survival skill.

Advances in technology increase the pace of daily life, and screen time is any time. Toddlers happily engage with electronic keypads. Young children deftly program computers (and often troubleshoot for their parents). Teenagers are immersed in social media, and adults are busy with their own tablets and devices. However, this fast pace and proliferation of screen time can override the good intentions of even the best multitaskers, far outreaching their capacity to cope with all the demands and resulting in delaying or even ignoring tasks and opportunities. Procrastination has seeped into the everyday landscape of social interaction and daily functioning.

Children need help determining what is potentially unsafe, what is not so critical (immediately or in the broader sense), and what they can realistically postpone or disregard. For example, parents who see their child spending too much time on tech devices often worry about it displacing other aspects of his life. Yet they may have a hard time convincing him to turn away from the screen. Power struggles often ensue when children and parents disagree on how time is—or should be—spent.

Power Struggles

Ongoing procrastination that has serious consequences may become a matter of daily drama and consternation where home becomes a battleground of sorts. A power struggle may start out mildly, but can quickly escalate to a standoff or a shouting match where emotions run high. Children may become belligerent and uncooperative and refuse to do something or to back down. Parents may feel frustrated, angry, and helpless in the face of such conflict. Confrontational situations can happen from toddlerhood through the teenage years and beyond.

Regardless of how a power struggle starts—and even that may be a point of contention—avoid laying blame and try to handle matters productively rather than defiantly. Children and parents do not always see things eye to eye and disagreements are a natural part of life. Power struggles can be de-escalated if parents take a calming approach. Here are 10 suggestions to try:

1. Take time apart. Don't allow yourself to be baited and drawn into non-productive arguments. "Taking the sail out of the

wind" (they are the wind and you are the sail) gives everyone time and space to collect their thoughts and let the emotions dissipate.

2. Consider silence to get a point across. Silence does not mean that you agree with what has been said.

3. Respect one another. Few things are as irritating to kids as feeling as if they are not being heard.

4. Be fair. Set expectations and timelines together. Strive toward two-way communication, rather than edicts.

5. If you set limits, make sure that you really intend to enforce them and that you can carry them out. Otherwise, you undercut your credibility.

6. Listen. Rephrase what you are hearing. Ask follow-up and clarifying questions to be sure you understand what your child means. ("Later" is a good word to define.)

7. Consider how you can praise your child in ways that encourage productive action or at least recognize previous accomplishment.

8. Where possible, let natural consequences occur (rather than ones you impose), and avoid saying "I told you so" if things don't work out well.

9. Keep your sense of humor. You are going to need it, and it will help you overcome feelings of resentment or hostility. Those can only be counterproductive.

10. Don't leave the air tense. Hug afterward. Make sure you both feel open to further dialogue and the child knows that your love is unconditional.

When a power struggle escalates and gets out of hand, a situation or a relationship can start to destabilize. Professional counseling may be called for. Power struggles can also lead to recurring procrastination. There may be other issues as well, such as stress or depression.

In these cases, a family doctor, psychologist, or guidance counselor can provide direction.

Powers struggles that lead to task avoidance may be occasional and not overly serious. Solving the problem then might involve devising checklists, interim finish lines, or a creative system of color-coding action steps.

Different temperaments prompt different behaviors and responses. Personas of procrastinators vary (as noted in Chapter 1), but a person's character is uniquely her own. Temperament refers to the inborn traits that influence how we respond to experiences, including those that are challenging or unexpected.

Psychologist Jerome Kagan has researched children's temperament and how it can be influenced by genetic dispositions and environmental factors. He identified two primary types of temperament, inhibited (timid, shy, and possibly fearful) and uninhibited (sociable, outgoing, and willing to take risks).[116]

A child's temperament could affect whether or not she will engage in power struggles, fret over small worries, effectively juggle daily responsibilities, be task committed, or be more inclined to avoid tasks. However, a child's interactions with her surroundings are always in flux. Temperament tends to be stable, but a person can learn to overcome or change it to some degree. For instance, parents can help a child develop a more easy-going or even a bold temperament. (The down side is that too easy-going might mean less responsible, and too bold might be disrespectful. It can be hard to find that sweet spot.)

No matter how much parents model, talk about, and encourage productive behavior, some people procrastinate because that is just their way. It is how they function, from time to time, or day to day—for better or worse.

Figure 9.1. Tips for Preventing Power Struggles and Procrastination

○ **Anticipate triggers**. Be alert to situations that are getting out of hand, and make the effort to de-escalate them before they erupt and become even harder to manage. Try not to fume or yell.

○ **Calm, Alert, and Ready to Learn.** This is a self-regulation program that helps children learn to calm themselves if they are feeling stressed or having difficulty coping with what is happening in their lives.[117] There is considerable literature about this program, and it is being used successfully in many places in North America, New Zealand, and elsewhere.

○ **Consider the upside and the downside.** Help kids learn to do a "cost analysis" of sorts. Make a list: What are the benefits of doing something? Of not doing it? What are the drawbacks of doing it? Of not doing it? Seeing it written down can help kids decide what needs doing sooner rather than later.

○ **Reduce screen time.** Lots of kids—and parents—struggle with this one. The fact remains that too much time spent on personal devices means less time to spend on other things. Help kids recognize when they are experiencing tech overload or when it is interfering with their productivity.

○ **Pick battles wisely.** Is confrontation really necessary? Is it worth the impending hassle? Is the problem likely to subside on its own? Whose problem is it? Sometimes stepping back from the front lines provides a new and valuable perspective.

Messiness! Chores! Homework!

Over the course of my work, I have spoken to countless parents about procrastination, and three specific areas of concern bubble to the surface again and again. It seems that kids can be rather notorious for procrastinating when it comes to 1) dealing with messiness, 2) following through with chores and responsibilities, and 3) doing homework and assignments. Why is that? And what can parents do about it? These concerns tend to be common among tweens and teenagers, but are not confined to these age groups. Let's consider practical strategies for each of these three topics.

Messiness

Among the many perils of pre- and post-puberty (especially but not exclusively) is one that *parents* experience—the clutter and mess that kids inevitably seem to generate. Many parents are dismayed to see their teenagers' rooms with clothes everywhere except on hangers in the closet. Books, papers, and other items lie helter skelter. Teens love to have their own space, except once they do, it can turn into a sea of electronic gizmos, sports equipment, and who-knows-what else. Often this muddle morphs into a bigger mass, infiltrating other rooms, and spreading out until it threatens to take over the whole house. "I'll clean it up later!" is a refrain uttered by kids in thousands of households every day.[118] Should parents just sigh resolutely and sidestep the clutter and the issue? Does it help to nag kids or give them ultimatums?

It is wise for parents to pick their battles in deciding what is totally unacceptable (such as moldy, wet towels strewn on the floor, or dirty dishes and crusty leftovers lying around attracting bugs), and what is tolerable (such as leaving electronics on the table, or clean laundry on a chair in their room, and other bearable sloppiness that family members can live with).

Conventionality says that an individual should look after his own possessions, preferably in ways that do not encroach on other people's space. Kids may know this but choose not to act upon it— quite possibly because it's just not important to them. We all know people who can walk past a crooked picture or a fallen candy wrapper and barely notice that anything is awry. Others immediately want to reach out and fix things. It is not always possible to radically change a non-interventionist type into a more proactive one, but it *is* possible to work toward making little changes, incrementally.

Some children do not clean up their messes because they are trying to assert their independence. But saying "I'll live my life my way!" can also be an expression of anger or rebellion toward parents deemed to be controlling.

Remember that you are helping your child to become self-reliant and to eventually possess the knowledge, skills, and experience to leave your home and survive. So coach toward self-direction and autonomy, rather than nag. Suggest a chat about possible solutions toward greater tidiness. A logical place to start is with the obvious clutter. Speak in a nonconfrontational tone about how and why it is upsetting to you, appeal to reason, saying something like, "I feel resentful when you leave a mess after I've asked you to clean up because it feels like you expect me to do it," or "I feel disappointed that there's clutter because I like the house to look neat when friends drop by." Offer to help set up a plan and give assistance for decluttering by providing garbage bags, a hamper, a vacuum cleaner, boxes, decorative baskets, closet organizers, or whatever else is needed. Use the words *please* and *thank you* liberally. Convey reinforcement once cleanup has started and while it is underway. Do not emphasize efficiency. It can put pressure on a child. Take pleasure in the fact that the process is underway even when it is slow. And believe it or not, some kids just outgrow this messy stage, though it may take years!

Be proactive yourself. Stay ahead of your own clutter. Discard or donate unworn or unnecessary items, and do not save junk or leave things lying around in heaps. Have designated spots for papers, clothes and accessories, and knick-knacks. Keep your desk clear to serve as a model of what an efficient work space looks like. Ask kids politely to appreciate the space that has been set aside just for them and to be considerate of others who see or walk through it. Some people are pack rats with strong emotional attachments to their things, and they may have trouble letting go of them, even if they do not use them any more. Show kids how to be charitable and where they can donate items to those who are less fortunate. Teach the art of sorting for organizational ease (outdated/current, useful/superfluous, clean/ dirty), the importance of recycling for the environment, and the courtesy inherent in returning things that belong to others. Look for creative spots for intelligent storage—in plastic or cloth containers under a bed, hanging in suspended nets or stacked cubicles, arranged on little shelves in corners or inside the closet, or maybe stashed in a designated place in a basement or apartment storage locker. Share the feeling of accomplishment one enjoys when looking at a newly cleaned drawer or floor area. Take a photo!

Don't make your cleanup request at an inopportune time—such as when children are bogged down with homework or too tired. If you ask them to spend just a few minutes each day instead of doing everything all at once, they will be less likely to procrastinate. You can also mention that even if they make a small effort to keep things tidier while in the throes of going about everyday activities, stuff might not pile up as much. When they are unsure about what to do with some objects that have accumulated, have them try a one-two punch—with phase one being to place those things in a large bin or bag to address in phase two after other things have been cleared away. Encourage kids to try doing the toughest or nastiest part of the job first. Getting that out of the way can be motivating.

Have children picture the success of an uncluttered space. Suggest they do the cleanup job while listening or singing along to music or talking on the phone. Have them use an air freshener. The smell can invigorate the senses and make a person feel more alert. Make straightening up into a game by setting a timer and seeing how much can be done in a given time frame, perhaps with a pre-established reward at the end, such as a treat, a movie, or something of their choice. Ask them to find as many unexpected, weird, or valuable items as they can within their clutter. Suggest that they use a mini-planner to write down what they can do to declutter—the first few steps at least. Seeing it in writing and then being able to check things off can act as incentive to continue.

Finally, try having kids reconfigure their thought processes, attitudes, or self-talk around tidying up. For example, if they are thinking "I'm being forced to clean my room," or "My parents are making me throw away my stuff," they likely feel that they are being subjected to someone else's will. Help them reposition their thinking along the lines of "I'm really doing this for me. My room is going to be way better once I get rid of the mess." Then it is not a matter of obedience or submission to someone else's demands. Above all, maintain your relationship.

The environment people create for themselves can be stifling and muddled, or it can be orderly and invigorating. Even young kids are old enough to understand the difference and may just need help to appreciate that they have a hand in making the right choices for their personal success.

Chores and Responsibilities

Kids are most successful when they have learned how to meet challenges and work hard. When parents shelter them from chores and responsibilities, it can compromise that learning. Whether it is walking the dog, clearing the kitchen table, or raking the leaves, kids can and should take some responsibility as part of the family. When they refuse or procrastinate, then things are left undone and people feel irritated. Over longer periods of time, tensions mount, and eventually there is a rift in the family dynamic.

The more frequent the procrastination, the greater the potential for rift. Parents who placate kids and allow them to abdicate their repsonsibilities do them no favors. When kids rebel, there is usually a reason. Maybe they have too much else going on. They may procrastinate around chores as a way to assert independence. They may also put off doing them because they got away with doing so in the past, or perhaps because they have friends who are not held responsible at home.

Perhaps try to work out a verbal or written contract that may lead to some sort of reward or trade-off. Parents might say, "I'll sort and run the the laundry if you'll help me fold and put it away please." Set out what the job entails and what the consequences are for non-compliance. In this situation, there would be no clean clothes and they would have to wear dirty, perhaps even smelly, clothes. Make it matter to them because when things don't matter, they don't get done.

Even very young children can handle suitable chores and simple tasks around the house, as was pointed out years ago by Maria Montessori who developed a chart listing age-approriate chores for children from age two through the teen years.[119] Small children can decorate the dinner napkins, pick up toys, and put their soiled clothes in a hamper. As they get older, children should be expected to contribute their time and effort in significant ways, such as organizing their school things so they are ready to leave on time in the morning.[120] Teens can help with cooking and can certainly put away the dishes. Parents who always look after all the household chores do their children a disservice because the children will need these life skills when they grow up and go off to college, secure a job, or get married.

Chores can be mutually decided upon (together or perhaps during family meetings), but the jobs should be fair and have a reasonable time frame.[121] The relevance of chores is important, too. Kids tend to be more responsible when their personal property or happiness is involved. They may procrastinate less and pay more attention to tasks that are related to their own lives and interests.

Help kids remember their chores by keeping a family planner in clear view. Post-it notes or a colorful weekly job wheel might be another approach. Let siblings trade off their responsibilities now and then, e.g., "I'll look after clearing the table if you'll take out the trash." Have a household routine for morning, after school, and evening, and that way everyone knows what needs doing when. That said, alarm clocks do not always go off, people sometimes feel under the weather, and kids can take longer than anticipated doing one thing and have difficulty getting started on another—so be flexible.

Homework and Assignments

Here are some school-related reasons why children procrastinate. These kids' comments were shared by parents whom I encountered at conferences, schools, and elsewhere.

"There's no ink in the printer, so it would be a waste of time to do a final draft."

"What I've written isn't good enough. I'll finish it later when I figure out how to make it better."

"If I do this too soon, I'll just have to redo it before it's due."

"I have too much other stuff to do."

"I work better under pressure."

"I have to find more information first—and process it."

"The teacher expects too much."

"I need more time to let my creativity flow."

"I can do it quickly, so it'll wait."

"I need to relax."

Kids' incomplete schoolwork is the bane of some parents' existence. Many parents become overly frustrated, convinced that procrasination will inevitably compromise their child's education. Parents may want to step in and make things better, but is that really wise? Children have to learn about the consequences of their actions. Let's say a teen puts off studying for a test and then does poorly on it. Of course, a parent should not say, "I told you so!" Instead, it would be more productive to be genuinely sympathetic and say something like, "I'm sorry you failed the test. I wonder, how can you plan ahead and manage your time so it's not likely to happen again?"

Homework can be a trigger for arguments and disappointment. On the other hand, it can also be a catalyst for developing good, productive work habits.

Is there a quiet place for study? Is homework part of the daily routine? Does your child understand the assignment? Does she know how to ask for help when something is unclear? Are the necessary materials handy? Is the homework meaningful?

Based on their past homework experiences, kids can figure out how much time to allot to their assignments. Creating a framework for action using a daily or weekly planner is a good idea. A written plan can be especially useful for meeting the demands of long-term assignments. Those are the ones that can be most problematic; kids may procrastinate because there is the illusion of lots of time, and because the work may seem overwhelming.[122] A plan might involve the following steps: 1) determine the exact number of days or work time available until the assignment is due; 2) divide the work into specific tasks—for example, organizing materials and resources, researching, writing drafts, revising, and finalizing, while still leaving one or two additional days for unexpected complications; and 3) check off each task as it is done to see proof of progress. Many kids find it helpful to create the list of tasks in the order they need to be done and to estimate how much time each will take. Then they can plan backwards from the due date to the current day to see if that plan will work. If it won't, or if interior deadlines are missed, the remainder of the plan can be adjusted. Always knowing the next step helps kids stay on track and helps avoid the illusion that "I finished the research-gathering so early that I can take some time before I start to write seriously."

When doing homework, kids can get bogged down and feel tempted to procrastinate. A timer can be useful for scheduling breaks. Setting a target amount of work to be done (e.g., complete Section 1 of the spelling or finish reading a chapter of the assigned reading) may work better for kids who do not like using a timer. Regular time-outs can help build momentum and prevent a sense of overload. If kids have questions, they can also call a homework hotline. And do not expect children to nose-dive into their homework immediately after a full day at school. Give them a chance to unwind first, to play, to enjoy a snack, or to spend time with friends and family. Many kids have days that are jam-packed, and homework is yet another task they have to juggle.

Some students have the entrenched atttitude that homework is simply a useless burden, as echoed in the oft heard "Homework sucks." Although homework is not a parent's responsibility, it may be helpful to offer some initial guidance or clarify expectations, particularly at the beginning of a school year. However, if assignments are not done, it is not a parent's job to do them. Parents have to stay united on this front. Dad may be great at writing and mom may be a math whiz, but they do not have to hand in the work or show that they understand the concepts. Homework is meant to extend and consolidate children's learning, and kids have to be accountable for that, as well as for what happens when they procrastinate or disregard their work. Consequences may vary from teacher to teacher and subject to subject, or even in the way any one teacher handles homework avoidance from the beginning of the year to the end. These mixed messages can influence whether a student feels inclined to work or not.

Parents can help kids learn to assert themselves respectfully and to develop good questioning skills so they can inquire politely if they do not understand something about the homework. It may be useful for them to ask about—and establish the relevance of—what has been assigned, to find out whether there is any due date flexibility, and to learn the consequences for lateness. Parents should offer to meet with the teacher when necessary to maintain communication channels and prevent misunderstandings between home and school.

Another strategy is to introduce interesting vocabulary and challenging concepts to help them frame their thinking. For example, consider the word *conscientiousness*. The dictionary defines it as acting carefully, methodically, and in accordance with one's conscience. In practice, it means following through with a task you agreed to. Parents can teach kids about being conscientious by mentioning tasks they are responsible for at work, at home, or in the community, and then demonstrating follow-through until the tasks are finished. Introduce other words and their meanings—peppering the collection with fun words as well as those relating to productivity—and make connections to real situations wherever possible. Talk about how words are important, but how actions speak loudly, too.

Finally, do not forget that when it comes to helping children overcome procrastination with their assignments and homework, teachers are allies and valuable resources. As part of their professional training, they are taught educational psychology.[123] This encompasses child development, cognitive and behavioral considerations, and information about how students learn. It is part of a teacher's job to encourage and assist children who need support to get started on activities and stay engaged. Teachers should also welcome parents' questions. So if your child is being bombarded with what seems to be an unreasonable amount of homework day after day, contact the teacher and have a respectful, non-confrontational chat about this. When parents, teachers, and kids work collaboratively, it is a win-win-win scenario.

CHAPTER 10
Getting on Track

"The secret of getting ahead is getting started. The secret of getting started is breaking your complex overwhelming tasks into small manageable tasks, and then starting on the first one."
~Mark Twain

New developments in neuroscience continue to increase understandings of how the brain works. Over time, this information will provide additional answers to questions having to do with how people function, including the topics of learning, motivation, productivity, and even procrastination. This chapter provides some brain-related ideas for parents to use now in order to help kids get on track and stay there.

Another focus within this chapter is goal-setting. Why is it important? How can children learn to set goals they will want to reach? First we discuss some brain matters, and then we will focus on goals.

A "Head" Start: Brain Matters

The brain is always active and undergoing change. This is true whether a person acts consciously or unconsciously, whether the thinking or the emotional parts of the brain are called into play, and whether an individual's responses are connected to facts, fears, influences, or impulses.

There are some interesting findings in the field of brain research relating to teaching, learning, and procrastination. When a person feels strong emotions such as anxiety, intimidation, or embarrassment, the brain creates a filter that prevents new information from entering so that it can spend its energy on resolving the current stressful situation.[124] However, when a person perceives something pleasant, the brain "tunes in," enhancing the efficiency and speed of information flowing into its memory consolidation and storage areas.

Parents can help children maintain a balance between experiences that are taxing and those that aren't, between activities that are stimulating and those that are less rigorous, leaving time for thoughtful processing of information. Parents can also ensure that kids have enough sleep because the brain needs ample time to rest and consolidate thoughts and memories. A rested brain is also better equipped to cope with stress whether it is mental, emotional, or physical.

Researchers are investigating the science of delay—including cognitive and neural mechanisms, and connections to decision-making and emotional health.[125] Parents can help kids learn to pay attention to their own physiological functioning. That is, how their bodies respond when having to make decisions, meet demands, and confront stressful situations, and how difficult conditions might cause them to tune out or become less responsive. Bodily self-awareness enables children to become more attuned to how they react to challenges and to the kinds of strategies that will enable them to calm down and become more resolute. Such strategies might include deep breathing, yoga, and other relaxation techniques that can alleviate tension so they become focused and ready to function efficiently.[126]

Mood can affect productivity, and certain chemicals in the brain help to regulate mood. Serotonin is a neurotransmitter that helps defend against depression and anxiety. It is possible to keep serotonin levels up by consuming enough protein.[127] Proper nutrition nourishes the body, and the brain benefits, too. Parents have more say about what children eat when they are younger, but older kids can learn what foods enable them to function more effectively throughout the day. For example, experts will tell you that students who eat a good breakfast are better equipped to handle a morning's work than kids who miss breakfast or regularly consume sugary or baked treats. Aside from the fact that too much sugar is known to lead to health problems (including weight gain, tooth decay, heart disease, and diabetes), it can also compromise brain activity. When a child consumes a lot of "fast sugar" all at once, it can result in a rush, making it hard for him to concentrate.

Protein is a performance booster, and children can eat protein-rich food in the morning and throughout the day. It metabolizes slowly, leading to more stable blood sugar and insulin levels, so children do not feel hungry as quickly. When their blood sugar gets too low, they feel listless and hungry, which also makes it difficult for them to concentrate. Their energy is affected and their productivity declines. They do not feel like doing things and will put them off.

Foods that contribute toward more efficiency include protein-rich items like eggs, cheese, nuts, and yogurt. Foods to avoid include caffeine, sugary snacks, and sodas, all of which are known for giving a rush and then a letdown. Parents can adopt healthy eating habits and ensure that there are sufficient nutritious foods on hand in the fridge and pantry so children can make smart choices about what to eat. Parents can talk about the reasons for eating wholesome meals and offer to create some recipes together—ones that the family will want to eat and that will help maintain strong energy levels so they can function at their best.

Mood management has a lot to do with energy levels. When a child is cranky or resentful she is less likely to be compliant or to feel as if she is raring to go. We all work best when we feel energized. Have children track their energy levels at different hours of the day and night and then determine whether they have slump times and efficient times. Once these are charted, parents can respect kids' up-and-down mood changes.

The brain consists of many parts, but the executive-function part of the brain in the frontal lobe is a kind of neural control center. Some of the jobs or processes that require "executive" management include initiating tasks, processing and responding, attending and sticking to tasks, and shifting from one activity to another. This part of the brain is also involved in activities such as regulating feelings, building upon previous learning, and anticipating and planning for the future.[128] People who have difficulty with executive functioning are likely to procrastinate. Perhaps it is getting started, directing focus, or transitioning between tasks. A good start for an individual seeking to get and stay on track would be to determine what specific areas of executive functioning need careful consideration, and then to work on one executive functioning challenge at a time. Whether it is staying focused, recalling facts, or something else, identify and tackle one area of difficulty before moving on to another.

Perhaps one of your children has difficulty remembering instructions, whereas another has trouble with organization. They both put things off. When a person recognizes what is leading to procrastination, she is better able to address the issues and resolve them. If it involves memory, developing a system of jogs or mnemonic schemes for remembering will help. If it is an organizational problem, some creative desk-straightening ideas may be the answer. For example, try colorful boxes, plastic dividers, bright labels, alligator clips, woven baskets, cloth bins, and shelving units for under, over, and beside the desk. Encourage kids to stash things by subject area, to throw out outdated papers and keep a garbage can handy, and to place the most important or time-sensitive items uppermost and easily accessible. Of course, strategies will vary depending on the situation, the difficulty in question, age level, and whether the person is willing to confront and resolve the matter. Parents can talk with kids about possible strategies and encourage them to think about teaming up with someone who has strong executive functioning in areas where they could use a boost.

Portnoy studies and writes about delay, and he explains how one part of the brain responds quickly and automatically in the short term, whereas another part responds more deliberately in the long term. He discusses the neurological implications of procrastination—that is, how brain function relates to immediate and future preferences.[129] Implications of this sort can help to inform understandings of why and when people behave as they do in response to tasks. Pioneering and exciting brain research is being conducted all around the world. For example, in Toronto, a "virtual brain" has recently been developed—a computerized model that presents an open simulation of how the brain works.[130] Increased knowledge about the brain will continue to lead to innovations in different disciplines and to cutting-edge applications for learning, medical care, and behavior.

There is no reason why kids cannot learn the basics of how the brain operates and begin to comprehend and appreciate this incredible organ.[131] Carol Dweck has developed a program called *Brainology* used in schools across North America and elsewhere. This program raises students' achievement levels by helping them develop a growth mindset, by teaching them how people learn and remember, and by describing how the brain changes when exercised.[132] The program also focuses on brain research, including what is new. The bottom line is that children recognize how they can affect their own learning through effort, persistence, and motivation. This in turn can affect their academic success and potentially their success in other areas of life, such as careers and relationships. Parents can adapt the *Brainology* program for use at home to help children gain an understanding of the brain and harness their competencies.

Here are some other brain-based strategies to help kids overcome procrastination:

Figure 10.1. A "Head" Start to Beat Procrastination

○ **Enrich children's lives with language, music, and movement activities.** Language, music, and movement can improve children's cognitive development, including better developed and coordinated neural networks.[133] Enhanced capacities translate into more efficient learning, as well as more excitement about learning. This can generate a "get right down to it" approach.

○ **Be curious.** Curiosity is a fundamental part of learning. Help kids hone their inquiry and thinking skills. Asking who, what, where, when, why, and how can get them engaged. Teach them how asking questions, beginning with their own areas of interest, can connect them to a subject they previously chose to ignore. When actively involved in a task, they are more likely to stay committed.

○ **Encourage ample downtime, within reason.** This includes time for quiet introspection, innovation, mind wandering, and exploration at a leisurely pace. Knowing there is quality time for this, children learn to focus more pointedly when they have to direct their attention, get to work, or complete the more serious learning required of them.

○ **Lighten up.** Try not to be consistently demanding. High attention can be stressful. Break it up. Chill.

○ **Encourage poetry, art, dance—whatever stimulates the senses.** These pursuits can work to activate parts of the brain and help invigorate a child. A person who is alert and feels energized is more likely to apply himself *now*.

○ **Reduce screen time.** Rampant social media can rob kids of time to read books, think, complete homework, participate in sports, and so on. Guide and encourage them in making responsible screen time decisions and working their way toward independence.

○ **Be organized.** Help kids find organizational strategies that work, ideas or tips they might want to try, or suggestions found online or elsewhere. Brain-building is not only about *acquiring* information; *organizing* it is important, too.

○ **Model calm, purposeful resolve.** Demonstrate a focused, measured approach to learning and doing. Parent procrastinators can try some of these strategies. Parents who discern what they do well—and what they can aspire to do more efficiently or effectively—are better able to teach children to do the same.

○ **Offer direct, immediate feedback.** It can spur momentum and keep kids interested so they don't go off task. Constructive, sensitive, and meaningful comments will help them stay productive and help their minds to stay active. Praise the effort and not just the result.

○ **Revisit the to-do list.** Perhaps a child's to-do list needs a little revamping, clarifying, or downsizing. Sometimes a visual representation is the way to go to crystallize intentions or processes. Some kids like to see a plan of action like a pictorial road map.

○ **Help children practice goal-setting.** You will find ideas in the next section.

○ **Appreciate that motivation is influenced by how imminent a reward might be.** The farther away the reward, the more likely kids are to discount its value. Similarly, if a deadline is distant, it seems less pressing. Knowing about this "temporal

discounting" characteristic sheds light on avoidance and procrastination behavior, and supports the importance of setting
intermediate goals as well as long-term ones.[134]

Goal-Setting

Why is goal-setting important? Psychologist Maureen Neihart
writes, "The simple act of assigning a challenging goal can raise a child's
confidence because it communicates an expectation and a confidence
that the individual has the ability to accomplish the task. That's why it's
important to keep the bar high while providing support and guidance...
Review goals often to keep focused, and adjust effort or strategy."[135]

Goals should be attainable and purposeful. It also helps if a goal is
specific—not broad-based or vague. A parent might say, "Please clean
up the backyard." Instead, it would be better to say, "Please rake the
leaves," or "Please pull any weeds in the garden," or "Please water the
flowers." A goal is more realizable if there are distinct steps to take. It
also helps if the goal can be reached in a timely fashion, that is, not
so far into the future as to seem too distant to bother.

Goals can be set independently or co-created with parents,
teachers, schoolmates, or others. The people and influences in a child's
life will have a bearing on whether kids will procrastinate in trying to
reach goals. They can also affect whether or not a goal will ultimately
be attained.

Once a goal is set, the question becomes *how* to attain it—how
to translate intentions into action. If it is relevant and makes sense to
the child, there is a better chance that he will be conscientious about
trying to reach it. You can say, "The gardening tools are in the garage.
The backyard is going to look awesome once it's all straightened up.
Maybe we can have a picnic afterward!"

Keep in mind that children have different pacing requirements
when it comes to schoolwork, home-based responsibilities, or goal-at-
tainment. Some kids need or prefer lots of time to carefully think
through things before they begin, as well as during, and even after.
Others quickly zip through an activity or chore if, or once, they get
going. Still others may not be able to gauge how long it is going to take
them to complete an assignment or task, and so they may procrastinate

and find they do not have enough time at the end. They may never reach their intended goal, but they may reach interim ones along the way, and learn a lesson for next time.

Parents can encourage kids to think back on previous experiences in order to see how long it took them to finish a similar task, and then suggest that they apply that knowledge as they confront a new one. Once children know how much time they actually need to do a task based on their own past experiences, they may be better able to pace themselves.[136]

A goal may be suitable for one child and yet not for a classmate or sibling. If a goal is a "good fit" with respect to pacing, degree of difficulty, intrigue, and relevance, then a person will be more inclined to tackle it.

Parents can ask kids to think about why some goals are more appealing than others. Longer timelines for completion? Fewer steps involved? Less decision making required? Sounds like fun? Neither too easy nor too hard? Kids have a sense of what their capabilities are, and some may have a tougher time accepting their limitations. Parents can help kids develop whatever skill sets might be needed to achieve their goals. Setting a series of small goals with interim manageable deadlines may be the best approach for a particular child. Sometimes an individual has lots of demands to deal with at once. Staggering them may be a possibility. Encourage him to think about prioritizing. Which goals are most important and why? Which ones have some flexibility, such as a longer grace period before the deadline? What are the consequences if a particular goal is not attained? Who is counting on him to have something completed? Figuring out the answers to questions like these can reduce some of the pressure and uncertainty about what to do when tasks pile up. For example, studying for the math exam this week may be essential, whereas the essay due at the end of the month can wait. Doing one's share for the group presentation tomorrow is a commitment that matters because people are depending on it. However, finishing an independent science report for a teacher who offers flexible due dates is likely not as pressing.

If a goal or task seems daunting, it may be helpful for kids to watch how others go about attaining it. This can serve as a primer and as incentive. Sometimes competition can motivate kids. Parents and teachers have to be careful that a competitive environment is comfortable and that the child feels the particular goal is attainable, as oposed to being something unreachable or stress-inducing. It is best if the child has a supportive milieu—one that is safe, respectful of her abilities, reinforcing, motivating—and that the goals or tasks she is asked to complete are appropriate and doable. Talking to kids about individual differences and paying attention to the fact that there are many dimensions of diversity between people will help them to feel more at ease in competitive situations.

Finally, when children set goals, with or without the assistance of adults, it is good for them to learn to stay focused. Help them be very specific when thinking about *what* they hope to achieve and *how* they plan to achieve it. In order to get on track (and hopefully stay there), they can put their intentions in writing or drawings. Staying focused is an acquired skill. We all veer off course from time to time, and this is not necessarily a bad thing. However, in order to get things done it helps to have a plan, an end-goal, and the support of others who have confidence in your ability to succeed.

Figure 10.2. Goal-Setting: Putting Procrastination in Its Place

○ **Show genuine appreciation for children's curiosity, exploration, and diligence.** This can reinforce their desire to become actively involved in doing things rather than putting them off.

○ **Encourage kids to eliminate typical distractions for periods of time.** Video games, phone calls, e-mails, television, and snacks can all be deterrents.

○ **Expect setbacks.** Obstacles are inevitable and progress is not a straight line. Help kids learn to anticipate hurdles and to try and factor in the time, effort, and resilience that will be required to overcome them.

○ **Consider the messages conveyed.** Some parents regularly ask their child, "Have you started your homework?" "Are you doing your homework?" or "Have you finished your homework?" Aside from the fact that this can become very annoying to a child, he may also think, "My parents always look after my scheduling so I don't have to take that responsibility for myself." If kids don't develop accountability for themselves or for managing their time, they will have difficulty setting and striving for goals.

○ **Develop routines.** Kids need to become famliar with a routine and settle comfortably into it by themselves. Goals are more readily reached when there is consistency around what is expected.

○ **Let kids set a pace that works for them.** Bear in mind that there are times of the day when they tend to work more efficiently than others.

○ **Buddy up.** Sometimes kids work best with a buddy or group in order to get things done.

○ **Check out the neighborhood.** What is being offered at camps, extracurricular programs, and community centers in the area? There are often exciting learning programs or short sessions that combine fun and recreation with attention to skills acquisition or work habits.[137]

○ **Try a short cut.** It is not necessarily a cop-out. A short cut may be a worthwhile and efficient approach—provided it doesn't compromise quality. Striving to reach a goal the long way (e.g., reinventing the wheel or unnecessarily spending hours creating something from scratch) can eat up a lot of time and energy. A child who has put off the job of baking something for the school fair may be wise to use an instant cookie mix.

○ **How much does punctuality really matter?** Is it integral to the particular goal the child is facing? Decide whether there is some degree of flexibility, and if so, how much.

CHAPTER 11

The Five *Ms*

"It is never too late to be who you might have been."
~George Eliot

If you want to know more about what underlies children's procrastination tendencies and how to encourage a sense of industry, think about the following five influences: 1) mastery, the nature of challenge, 2) mindset, the importance of effort, 3) metacognition, the value of reflection, 4) meaningful relationships, the impact of interaction, and 5) motivation, the power of incentive. These influences are at the heart of this chapter on daily cadences of action and inaction.

Mastery Orientation: Challenge!

What is the difference between *adequacy, proficiency,* and *mastery?* Does your child know? The best way to find out is to ask. And perhaps consider this story.

Twelve-year-old Pauline had a week to complete an English assignment. Her class had been studying descriptive language, and now everyone had been asked to describe a "day in the life" in a place of their choice—a long stretch of sandy beach, a rocky crest, a farmer's field, an icy pond. It was up to each person to choose a locale and a season and to provide a full description of what it looked like, along with what they knew or imagined occurred there from noon one day to noon the next.

Pauline thought the assignment was rather pointless because she did not think anything ever happened on a rock or in a field. And a full day? Boring! How would she find enough words to fill up the required two pages? She had no interest in doing the work, so she procrastinated.

A couple of days before the assignment was due, the teacher went around the room and asked each of the students what place they had chosen. They were excited to tell about their choices, and the places were quite varied—a busy intersection, a castle moat, a deserted island, a pigsty, a golf course, and a swamp. No two were alike. The teacher came to Pauline, who was just starting to get intrigued by the choices others had made. Not wanting to admit that she still had not chosen, she had to come up with something really fast. "The children's playground in the little park across the road from my house," she said. "Great idea!" said the teacher.

Now Pauline was stuck. With only two days to go, she had to figure out what to write about a place she had not visited since she was a young child.

Pauline thought that maybe she could describe the swing sets, tell about a few of the kids who went on the slides and played on the grass, and mention the adults who watched them. And she would say that the park was empty at night. She could throw in some adjectives, add something about the sun and stars, and indicate that the park was a happy and bustling place during the day, but was very quiet once it got dark.

That would be *adequate*.

Later that day, Pauline began to think about what was in the park besides playground equipment, children, and their caregivers. There were animals, insects, maintenance workers, and joggers. She could describe what they did there, and she wondered how the various activities differed hour by hour. She pictured how the people looked and imagined what they might say to one another. She looked out the window at the playground and realized that the trees shading it were quite beautiful and that there were lots of colorful flowers near the benches next to the sandbox area. Maybe the flowers closed up at night, but there were lights that shone on the pathways, so maybe not. She could write about all of this.

That would be a *proficient* and interesting descriptive piece.

Pauline thought further and jotted down some of her impressions about the park. Then after peering out the window again, she decided to walk across the road and get a closer look at what was happening there. She watched the kids playing on the climbing wall and noticed how the neon paint shone brightly in the sunshine. She smelled the freshly mowed grass, spotted a robin's nest, heard laughter as children created pastel chalk drawings on the sidewalk, and noticed the little plaques beside the memorial trees that lined the walkway. One of them was for a dog named Scrappy. Pauline talked to some of the kids and asked them what they liked best about the playground area. She decided that later she was going to set up a tape recorder and record all the sounds of the park, including those that occurred at night. She sat on a bench and made some more notes about what she was seeing and feeling.

That would be a *masterful* descriptive account.

As Pauline thought more about the assignment and became increasingly excited about it, she no longer wanted to procrastinate. She collected details, used all her senses, tapped her creativity, and could not wait to write the piece. In fact, she even included a cover page with a drawing of the park. When she handed it in, she felt proud of her accomplishment and more aware of her own neighborhood than she had before. She realized that she had not only enjoyed the learning experience, but had pushed herself to make it unique and to make it the best it could possibly be.

Discuss with your child the meaning of success, how it comes in different guises and differs from person to person. Help children recognize and feel good about little achievements as well as bigger ones. Teach them to be wary of languishing in a comfort zone because "no one improves by repeating what he has already mastered."[138] So encourage your child to get out and explore, to exercise body and mind, to find something new to learn and then really learn it, to be a maverick, to ask questions, to be persistent, and to enjoy the process.

Mindset: The Effect of Effort on Accomplishment and Ability

I attended a presentation by Carol Dweck at a private school in Toronto. Hundreds of people, parents *and* students, filled the auditorium.[139] Dweck talked animatedly about intellectual growth. It seemed to me that everyone left with a more positive attitude about learning, a better understanding of brain-related functions, and a deeper appreciation of the power of persistence.

Dweck began the presentation by explaining the difference between a fixed mindset—intelligence seen as a fixed trait that you are either born with or not—and a growth mindset—intelligence seen as a malleable quality that can be developed over time with effort. She described intelligence as "a platform from which you grow." She showed pictures illustrating how neural plasticity works. She talked about how the brain changes and evolves in response to experience, and how this enables people to learn. According to Dweck, the key to learning—and doing—is to acquire and sustain a growth mindset.

How can adults model growth-mindedness for their children? Dweck laid down three fundamental rules.[140] The first is to *continue to learn*. Pay attention to experiences and think about them. Read and take part in study groups or book clubs. Attend conferences. Connect with a mentor or even become one. Actively pursue an interest you have harbored but never had a chance to pursue. Find new avenues for learning.

The second rule is to *work hard*. Effort carries people to the next level, and the next. Push past your comfort zones and strengthen your capabilities. Build upon what you already know. Don't give up. Continue to practice and apply yourself. Make it a priority to try some of the strategies here.

Rule number three is to *view setbacks as learning opportunities*. Do not see a deficiency or mistake in a negative light, but think of it as a chance to retool and strategize. Confront stumbling blocks and circumstances head-on. That way you develop resilience and the ability to recover more readily if difficulties arise later on.

By following these three rules and developing a growth mindset, people become increasingly motivated, and less likely to procrastinate. Parents can help children appreciate that what is easy can be boring because it is not a stretch, whereas what is challenging will prove to be more interesting and worthwhile.

Dweck also talked about the word *yet* as being a conduit for possibilities. Think about how this simple little word applies to procrastination. For example, if a child says, "I'm not doing this assignment," it is quite different from saying, "I'm not doing this assignment yet." The first assertion is definite, non-negotiable. The second leaves a distinct opening for some initiative. There is a sense that she *will* get it accomplished. Maybe with some support, it could be sooner rather than later. Parents who see *yet* as a positive indicator can encourage kids to strive toward reachable goals by thinking about what *yet* might mean to them. And if they don't want to do it quite yet, have faith that action and reflection can ensue as a result of cultivating a growth mindset.

Metacognitive Capacities: The Importance of Being Reflective

In Shakespeare's *Hamlet,* Polonius offers this bit of intelligence to his son Laertes: "This above all, to thine own self be true." These famous words have transcended time, perhaps because the sensible advice, conveyed from parent to child, gets to the heart of how to get through life.

The best way to be true to oneself is to get to know oneself. Self-knowledge comes about as a result of thinking, as well as thinking about thinking—which is called *metacognition.* Metacognition enables people to make connections with what they know and with previous experiences. It is also involved in the transfer of knowledge and skills from one subject area or activity to another. Kids can be helped to understand how their thinking processes work with examples. For instance, they can pick something they want to learn more about (guitar playing, water skiing, volcanoes, the North Star) and then think about what they need to know and how to go about acquiring the knowledge, step by step. Simply put, reasoning, comprehension, and problem solving are all part of metacognitive functioning. The thinking process is like a framework for action.

Can a person learn to control that thinking process? Absolutely! By thinking purposefully, not carelessly, and by organizing ideas. Pay attention to information, and plan, monitor, and evaluate progress. Parents can help kids foster reflective habits of mind by encouraging them to ask themselves questions: "How do I know if...?" "How did I get that answer?" "Would the same thing happen if...?" "When or why is it necessary to...?"[141]

Kids can also think about what kind of work is challenging, exciting, or upsetting. They can use that knowledge to gain awareness of when they work efficiently and when they procrastinate. Metacognitive processes can also help kids work through dilemmas, ponder options, question beliefs, and analyze details. Mulling things over more deeply can fire up their memories and stimulate them to make inquiries—all of which leads to increased learning.[142] Metacognition can also come in handy when kids are trying to determine the reasons for their procrastination. Thinking candidly and carefully about the *when*, *why*, and *how* of task avoidance can be illuminating.

Parents can help children learn to think in a focused manner by suggesting that they build upon previous projects or assignments that captured their imaginations. For example, "You know that colorful decoy you designed so birds wouldn't smash into the glass railings? Can you think of other ideas to prevent them from hitting the windows?" Talk with them about what they have been working on or reading, refreshing their recollections. Ask them a pointed question or two to encourage them to think more about or extend the material, such as, "Who was the author of that book you liked? What else has he written?" Encourage your child to keep a short log of what she recently found difficult, or ask her to think back to when she procrastinated or put something off altogether. E.g., "Why did that science experiment take so long?" or "What materials did you need when you created those models of how spiders spin their webs?" Then take a few minutes to ponder and chat about the log entries—what happened, what the items might have in common that could have led to the avoidance, and how she might have addressed it better. It is all about thinking in ways that will be productive!

Motivation: Intentions, Interest, and Personal Progress

What makes a task personally meaningful? According to educator Del Siegle, it is tied to the individual's identity.[143] If it is interesting or connects to the person's current experience or vision for the future, then it is deemed useful right now. Note the word *now*. If the task is not immediately useful or has no of-the-moment relevance, then it is primed to be relegated to *later*. Sometimes it is important to point out to the child how a task relates to something that is already meaningful to them and to make that connection.

Even a small accomplishment can be meaningful and act as a motivator. Dale Carnegie said, "Don't be afraid to give your best to what seemingly are small jobs. Every time you conquer one, it makes you that much stronger. If you do the little jobs well, the big ones will tend to take care of themselves."[144] Of course, nothing *really* takes care of itself, and there is much to be said for concerted effort and persistence. However, Carnegie had the right idea when he emphasized the importance of taking initiative, starting small, and letting motivation and successes build.

Motivation is linked to a person's view of his capabilities.[145] Kids can be helped to know and evaluate their strengths, and to recognize that they can bolster any skills that need work. Of course, it is always easier to do things that you already know how to do, and often more enjoyable, so developing or strengthening skills will likely be a challenge. As a result, bolstering may be less fun and more likely to lead to procrastination, but this can be tempered by assuring children that guidance, assistance, and other forms of support are close at hand. Parents should encourage their children's expectations of success as well as recognize and reinforce their efforts as they embark on activities and tasks—whether chores, school-based assignments, or other kinds of demands. Parents can also use motivation strategies to stimulate children's thinking and inquiry skills.

Parents are often concerned about incomplete schoolwork. Motivation to learn has a lot to do with finding enjoyment in understanding and accomplishment. That sense of joy affects how—or if—a child will choose to focus his attention, and how—or if—he will persist with a task. Motivation to learn can also be triggered by need (e.g., "I *have* to be able to find my way home."), instinct (e.g., "I know there's a faster way to do these equations."), or curiosity (e.g., "I wonder why penguins don't fly."). *Intrinsic* motivation is driven from within, elicits feelings such as pride and competence, and involves internalized values such as diligence and integrity.

What can parents do to boost this internal drive? Try bridging the unknown with what is known. A parent can say, "You already recognize that thunder and lightning go together, but why?" Or add in some controversy, contradiction, or suspense; for example, "Why are wasps more likely to sting than honey bees?"[146] Try active problem solving and activities that require playful exploration or conjecture, such as "Can't find your shoes? Where are they *not* likely to be? Where could they be hiding? Time to look!" Reinforcing a child's efforts and persistence can also increase intrinsic motivation. This can generate action, spark a search for information, and stimulate further curiosity. The goal is to encourage curiosity that will begin a search for knowledge.

Two key findings in the literature on motivation and academic success are: 1) Tasks should be meaningful; and 2) Tasks and ability level should match. A child's responses usually can serve as a barometer for applicability and challenge. If a child is truly bored and has tuned out, then the activity is likely too easy.[147] You can discuss how to notch it up and make it more challenging and appealing. If he says he is confused or frustrated, then that warrants some discussion about how to make the activity more doable so efforts will lead to accomplishment. A good rule of thumb is to avoid asking kids to memorize stuff or to do overly simplistic or repetitive tasks—sometimes referred to as "busy work" or "drill and kill."

Some parents use *extrinsic* motivators as incentives to reinforce or stimulate their children's efforts. For example, applause or appropriate praise can help build a child's self-esteem and prompt engagement in a task. Other motivators may include rewards, grades, or gold stars.[148] Incorporating a child's interests, hands-on activities, and direct assistance can also be motivating. However, whether any such motivator will actually work depends on many factors. These include the child's perceived complexity of the task, its relevance, whether he thinks the interim and ultimate goals are realistic, and the kind of pacing expected of him. He will probably think about his chance of success, perhaps based on similar past experiences. So on the one hand, parents may do their best to extrinsically motivate their child, and on the other, there are many hurdles the child can be envisioning that he will want to try and reconcile before he will buckle down. This may all take a while, and it might look from the outside like procrastination.

For the past 10 years, I have taught Educational Psychology to prospective teachers. Motivation is a major topic of discussion within this course, and I have to make sure that my classes are motivating, otherwise, what message would I be sending? We talk about extrinsic motivation as a stepping-stone to the development of intrinsic motivation—which in turn helps kids develop autonomy, create and sustain commitment, and learn to balance responsibilities and demands. Every year I ask the teacher candidates in my class to record their top 10 motivators. Then I use a rousing game format with a soft rubber ball as a directive, tossing it from person to person as they take turns sharing as many motivators as possible. Last year's cohort generated a total of 218 motivational ideas in about 45 minutes.[149] Many of them would be good for parents to use, too. Here are over 40 examples:

Recognition

Routine

Novelty

Choice

Enthusiasm

Collaboration

Fair assessment

Direct applicability

Fun factor

Gaining respect of peers

Physical activity

Breaking tasks into steps

Rewarding each step

Time and opportunity to work independently or with others

Healthy competition

Breaking a barrier or record

Fresh air

Being able to complete something in your own preferred way

Suitable depth of material

Becoming a role model or mentor

Humor

Outings

Learning something to the point where you can teach it

Sparking the spirit of invention

Interesting rubrics and marking schemes

Breaks and time out

Positive attitude

Inspirational quotes

Excitement

Connectivity to cultural experiences

Opportunities to socialize or play

Motivating speakers

Music

Creative instructional techniques

Constructive and honest feedback

Change of scenery or environment

Understanding why something is important and how it will be useful

Incentive of a leadership role

Acceptance

Opportunity to use technology

Rest

Open scheduling

Ensuring it's okay to make mistakes.

Other ideas that I added to the mix included:

Reasonable constraints	Encouraging inquiry and
Flexibility	creativity
Rules	Help dealing with organiza-
Surprise	tional aspects such as time
Respecting the unique qualities	management skills, reason-
of the individual	able deadlines, and interim/
	formative assessments.

Sometimes all it takes is to say something affirming, like "I know you can do this!" If parents are discerning, have a trusting relationship with their children, and can discuss matters honestly with them, then those words will resonate and serve to motivate, too.

Meaningful Relationships: What Matters Most?

Procrastination can pose problems for children and parents alike. When schoolwork is left undone and responsibilities like chores and homework seem to be piling up, tension often mounts. The home front can become a place where everyone is on edge.

The parent-child relationship is very special. A strong relationship is forged, not forced, and it is fostered by many factors, including love, open communication, sharing, thoughtfulness, mutual respect, trust, and understanding. These are the fundamental factors; others will vary from one family to another.

Some people have a permissive approach to parenting, sometimes bordering on indulgence. Others are very strict about matters, enforcing rules and establishing expectations with little or no wriggle room. Some parents are inconsistent, being rigorous one day and lenient the next, conveying mixed messages to kids about what they can and cannot do (or get away with). The research literature tells us that when parents find that comfortable middle ground where boundaries and limits are fair and enforced fairly, their children are well positioned to thrive.[150] Those kids are not about to test limits because they know what they are, and why they are set—and they're okay with that. There is an underlying foundation of security and trust.

Relationship-building strengthens the bonds between a parent and child. A meaningful relationship makes it safe for kids to try new things, knowing that someone supports them, and they are less likely to procrastinate. Kids who know their parents are on their side are more likely to feel at ease and venture out.

How can mothers and fathers fortify a parent-child relationship and ensure that it stays as strong as possible? Be available to listen and talk. Respond to questions with answers that are to the point and reasonable. Ask follow-up questions. If you do not know something, say so, and then work together with your child to find answers. Stay connected with what is important to your child—interests, feelings, achievements, and concerns. Inspire confidence. Start a dialogue and have fun together. Pay attention to what is going on in your child's life—the transitions, social networks, and academic highs and lows. Be consistent in how you approach discipline, setting sensible boundaries without being too controlling.

As a caring parent, it is natural to want to ask your child questions about what is bothering her. Make sure the questions you pose are answerable and relevant, not too intrusive, vague, or long-winded. Don't pepper her with a barrage or focus on too many things at once. Time your questions for when they are most likely to be answered willingly. Give advice when asked, keeping it short. Use texting, e-mail, and voice mail sparingly; it is better to speak in real time because tones in writing and recordings can be misconstrued. Take note if your child seems to be overwhelmed, stressed, or experiencing burnout. If that is the case, ease her into learning how to say *no* to the demands that don't matter so much, and help her to prioritize and schedule those that do. Don't assume you know what your child thinks is important, and don't be surprised if what she values most differs from what you value. For example, when it comes to writing an essay, what is most important? Is it timely completion, length, comprehensive content, intelligent use of resources, well-chosen focal points, or something else altogether? Your views and goals may be quite different from hers. Encourage downtime and work together to define the parameters of that. Don't wait too long to offer support and reinforcement. In other words, don't procrastinate. Adopt and convey an ongoing attitude of giving of yourself and helping.[151]

A child's relationships with peers are also important. The social aspect of school, including friendship circles, group activities, and classroom dynamics, can have a big impact on a child's productivity. If a child feels like she belongs to a learning community where her opinions and contributions are valued and she has a support network of friends who accept her for who she is and what she does, she will be more inclined to try tasks and be motivated to do well. Social acceptance and encouraging relationships can work to a child's advantage. Parents can stay attuned to their child's play and work communities, reinforcing positive behaviors, and showing children how to support and motivate one another.

Relationships with family members play a pivotal role in motivating and affirming children's capabilities. Enlist the help of siblings, grandparents, aunts and uncles, cousins, etc. who all have a common interest—helping the child be productive, responsible, and resilient, so she can experience happiness and success both now *and* later.

CHAPTER 12

Thinking It Through and Resources, Too

"The way to get started is to quit talking and begin doing."
~Walt Disney

Many of the practical strategies in this chapter have been mentioned elsewhere in this book. However, they appear here as handy lists—one for adults and one for kids. Also in this chapter are brief stories about some well-known people who overcame procrastination, about what inspired them and what we can learn from their experiences. These strategies and stories might catapult you into creating some new procrastination-busting ideas of your own.

Suggestions for Parents

Figure 12.1. *Dos* and *Don'ts* for Parents

Dos for Parents

- ○ **Watch for red flags.** These include poor health, exhaustion, unkempt appearance, stomach- or headaches, and other signs that may indicate that a child is experiencing stress or is having a difficult time coping with the demands of daily life.

- ○ **Offer encouragement—without being gushy.** Be genuine and timely. For example, give anticipatory praise or positive reinforcement partway through a task or activity to grease the wheels of progress. You might say, "I admire how you persist and work to stay organized even when it's challenging."

○ **Avoid power struggles.** Procrastination can be problematic, but there is no point in fighting about it. Be consistent with messages and exercise patience. Adults need to strike a balance between standing their ground and being flexible. Be fair. Make time for open communication and active listening.[152]

○ **Encourage and model downtime.** Incorporate it into each day's schedule and stick to it.

○ **Be prepared to assist.** Have on hand any materials that will likely be required for schoolwork completion, such as markers, poster board, ink cartridges, folders, electronic chargers, batteries, calendars, and whatever else might be needed and used as an excuse if not readily available. This is particularly vital at the beginning of the school year, but it is always important.

○ **Tap the immediate circle.** Think about who can help support a child's industry and responsibility. Encourage children to accept and appreciate assistance from caring others in their lives, and to use that advice to develop confidence and strengthen capabilities.

○ **Allow kids time to do something special.** Perhaps they would like to sleep in or have their favorite fruit smoothie before embarking on an onerous task.

○ **Recognize children's developmental and age-related readiness.** Give instructions they will understand. Honor their capabilities, areas of weakness, interests, and temperaments.

○ **Help kids learn to prioritize what is most important.** Be able to explain *why*—if asked.

○ **Promote wellness behaviors.** These include physical activity, adequate sleep, a nourishing diet, and time for reflection. All of this will lead to better brain health and overall well-being.

○ **Keep calm and carry on.** Rise above any anger or impatience about a child's procrastination. It doesn't help a child when his parents get derailed, become sarcastic, pressure him, or act judgmentally.

○ **Consider using extrinsic motivators from time to time as incentives.** For example, work toward a special outing or treat, but draw a line at bribery, which is not a good idea.[153]

○ **Make a kid contract.** An informal contract can be a way for parents and children to come together and work out a mutually beneficial plan to curb procrastination. For example, a child may agree to do a particular chore that he keeps avoiding (such as emptying his overflowing garbage can). In exchange for ongoing cooperation, he could be given an opportunity to do something he would appreciate, but that his parents keep avoiding (such as taking him to his favorite pizza place—the one that offers all those really weird toppings).

○ **Imagine.** Visualize jumping off a very high diving board for the first time. It can be scary—something to postpone. Now imagine yourself trying it and succeeding. The next time, it may be easier, and the time after that, easier still. Kids may need help getting acclimatized to tasks or activities. After the first couple of attempts, it often starts to feel fine, and then they may want to jump right in. Parents can help kids look past the immediate moment and see the satisfaction that lies beyond.

○ **Be polite.** Say *please* and *thank you* when asking kids to do something.

○ **Set expectations that are fitting and realistic for each particular child.** Treating children equally is not always fair. Just because one child needs braces on her teeth doesn't mean that parents should require all of their children to wear braces.

○ **Learn about self-regulation.** Kids may have to reframe their intentions so they become more doable. Show kids how to chunk a task into manageable blocks and assign a workable timeline to each one. Children can take short recesses and reassess their progress chunk by chunk.

○ **Talk about procrastination.** Procrastination is not necessarily shameful or disreputable. Help a child understand and deal with procrastination by talking about it candidly—the ups *and* downs.

Don'ts for Parents

○ **Don't be a pest.** Try not to nag or natter about what still has to be done. Focus on what has been accomplished and make note of the effort expended.

○ **Don't assume that a child's procrastination is willful disregard.** There are many reasons why children procrastinate, and some of them are sensible.

○ **Don't make comparisons.** Parents shouldn't compare a child with her siblings, friends, or any adult's younger self. Inspirational anecdotes used as incentives may work, but direct comparisons that make children feel devalued can be degrading and counterproductive.

○ **Don't be a micromanager.** Supporting and encouraging children is very different from trying to control their behavior.

○ **Don't be unyielding.** Show some sensitivity and flexibility by coming to terms with the reality that not everything gets done quickly or even at all. (Honestly—who gets 100% of tasks accomplished expediently?)

○ **Rein it in.** Don't embarrass, belittle, ridicule, or humiliate a procrastinating child. Words, actions, and sometimes even a tone of voice can be demeaning.

○ **Avoid broad goals.** Instead of saying, "Do your homework!" try saying, "Why not get started on the first few questions and see if you can get those done in the next half hour before taking a bit of a break." Better to be specific and even work in a positive angle if possible.

○ **Don't get *too* revved up about a child's interests.** If a child expresses an interest in something (saxophone, scuba diving or whatever), don't mow her down. Likewise, don't go into high gear, pressing for lessons and accomplishments. Keep demands off the table. Rent the instrument or equipment until she is serious about the pursuit. If she procrastinates or moves on to something else, so be it. Interests may be passing fancies and can change over time.

○ **Don't hover.** Stay attuned to the child. Keep in touch with the teacher. Know what is happening with extra-curricular programs and social relationships, but don't intrude unnecessarily. As much as possible, let the child lead the effort.

○ **Don't ignore the suggestions for children that follow here.** Kids can take responsibility for their actions and efforts, and parents can help motivate them.

Suggestions for Children

Figure 12.2. *Dos* and *Don'ts* for Children

Dos for Children

○ **Find someone you trust.** If an activity, task, or goal makes you feel uncomfortable, talk about it with an adult you can depend upon to listen, appreciate your concerns, and provide guidance.

○ **Believe in yourself.** Have faith in your own capabilities and self-worth.

○ **Get used to a routine.** You will be less inclined to stray off course and may feel decidedly more comfortable sticking with what is familiar and established.

○ **Look after yourself.** Eat well, get enough sleep, and give yourself time to relax and to play. You will be able to function more effectively than if you are tired, malnourished, or wound up.

○ **Be attuned to your own energy levels.** Think about when and why you are at your peak, and when and why you may seem lethargic, and then try to do things according to when you function best.

○ **Think about what motivates you.** Visiting friends? Playing outside? How can you use those motivators to your advantage?

○ **Think about how you waste time.** Watching reruns? Talking endlessly on the phone? How can you eliminate temptations like these?

○ **Speak up.** Don't be afraid to ask parents, teachers, family members, and friends for help when you need it.

○ **Use organizers.** Get planners, timers, brightly colored file folders, clips, cork boards, checklists, electronic organizers, and calendars—whatever it takes to develop a sense of efficiency and to learn to follow timelines. Record due dates, events, upcoming family activities, etc. on the planner. Keep it handy. Refer to it often. Consider using a pencil so you can make changes. (Have an eraser!) Check things off once they are completed. Include "Breathe" on the list so you will have at least one item to check off. It'll feel good.

○ **Pursue your interests.** Think about how to schedule various demands so they don't get in the way of other activities that you *really* want to do. However, also think about how to schedule those activities so they don't interfere with your responsibilities.

○ **Reflect on your past experiences—especially times when you procrastinated.** Learn from them. What happened? What can you do differently next time?

○ **Collaborate.** Connect with friends, a study group, or people who can encourage you. If there is a sense that others are depending on you and have confidence in you, it will help keep you on track.

○ **Tackle one goal at a time.** It is hard to try and juggle too many things at once. Think one goal. Break it into steps and set manageable intervals of time.

○ **Be respectful of others.** Take a few moments to consider how your procrastination can have an impact on other people. It may be enough to spur you to act.

Don'ts for Children

○ **Don't be shy.** Ask for a hand or specific assistance or extra support if you think you need it.

○ **Don't let others bail you out.** When the going gets tough, try and show some determination and stay with it.

○ **Don't allow yourself to be distracted.** Make a list of what distracts you and post it somewhere visible. Is it toys? Technological gadgetry? Music? Snacks? Internet? Get into the habit of putting those things away when you need to focus. If they are out of sight and harder to reach, they will be less of a distraction.

○ **Don't lie.** Know your reasons for procrastinating, as well as your feelings about what you believe you realistically can and cannot do (with or without assistance).

○ **Don't underestimate the power of pacing.** Figure out how much time you will really need to complete something (again, with or without assistance). Then tack on a little more time— just in case.

○ **Don't reach too far at first.** Focus on the process and not just the product—set small goals and take them step by step.

○ **Don't settle for rushed sloppiness or half-hearted attempts.** You may be done now but sorry later. Put forth a strong effort and take pride in that. Try requesting a slightly later deadline if you anticipate you may need it in order to do a job well. There may be some flexibility. Then be sure to do the job well!

○ **Don't take on too much alone.** Share the load and support one another.

○ **Don't waver in your commitment.** Stay on course by moving forward—even though that can sometimes mean undoing a step so you can improve it or get back on track. Sometimes progress can mean backing up a little to get a better footing before taking another run at the goal.

○ **Don't be rude.** Even if you don't want to do something (or can't get started) and you are feeling cranky, avoid letting your feelings spill all over others who are trying to help. Take time to cool off if need be. Explain your reasoning politely.

○ **Don't get caught up in a power struggle**. Kids in power struggles with adults often come out on the short end.

○ **Don't forget to reward yourself.** A break, a treat, a stretch, a pep talk, a happy dance—after you start something and get partway through. Whatever will help you feel upbeat and recharge.

○ **Don't act impulsively.** There is something to be said for spontaneity, but it can interfere with getting down to the business of what you have to do and what you already have planned. If you are suddenly struck by a great idea that wasn't in the original plan, write it down and save it for later when you can give it better attention.

○ **Don't get yourself down.** Everyone procrastinates. Don't let your procrastination compromise your sense of self or own you. There are lots of things you and your parents can do to help you overcome it, including reading the success stories that follow here.

Success Stories and Tips from Those in the Know

There are countless people who have beaten the odds to become not only productive but prolific. Many have written about procrastination. What were the accomplishments of some of the famous individuals whose quotes appear within this book? What might have prompted their comments? How did these people overcome procrastination and become celebrated for their achievements?

Parents can share with children and teens interesting thumbnail sketches of successful, well-known individuals. Stories and quotes can inspire action, fortify will, illustrate determination, and point the way toward a positive mindset and a greater sense of industry. To that end, here are glimpses into the lives of four people whose words about procrastination appear in this book. You and your child can investigate the history of other noted achievers and learn what incentives bolstered their resolve.[154]

Mark Twain, *American author and humorist, 1835–1910*
In addition to the quotes by Mark Twain previously noted (on pages 1 and 131), this highly acclaimed author wrote the following advice that any procrastinator can take to heart, "Twenty years from now, you will be more disappointed by the things that you didn't do than by the ones you did do. So throw off the bowlines. Sail away from the safe harbor. Catch the trade winds in your sails. Explore. Dream. Discover." Twain did just this in his own life. He wrote profusely, but he also experienced and overcame severe financial problems. And if you think about the protagonists in *The Adventures of Tom Sawyer* and *The Adventures of Huckleberry Finn,* you will recall enterprising boys and many escapades. Sheer determination gave them the edge to succeed. Twain was much the same. He kept writing and writing, and made an indelible mark in the literary world.

Twain's incentive was *perseverance,* combined with finding what he really liked to do (communicate and write), honing his skills over time, and using different outlets—newspapers, books and public speaking—to convey his ideas.

Benjamin Franklin, *Printing entrepreneur, scientist, inventor, and politician, 1706–1790*
Benjamin Franklin (quoted on page 1) is famous for his kite experiment, wherein he literally got a handle on lightning and verified the nature of electricity. He also invented swim fins, bifocals, and the Franklin stove. He was one of five committee members who drafted the *Declaration of Independence* and one of 40 who signed the *American Constitution.* He sought to abolish slavery, and he was a strong environmental advocate, which was somewhat of a rarity back in his day. With all these interests and involvements, this man could not afford to dilly-dally. He said, "You may delay, but time will not," and "Lost time is never found again."

Franklin's incentive was *curiosity*, combined with a strong sense of purpose to pursue goals, find solutions, and make discoveries.

Emily Dickinson, *Poet, 1830–1886*

Emily Dickinson (see page 163) was an accomplished American poet who wrote over 1,700 poems. She was extremely shy and rarely went out in public. Some people think that being a recluse allowed her more time to focus on her writing, and on her thoughts and feelings. Very few of her poems were published during her lifetime, but later, once the full breadth of her work was discovered and published, her powerful and unique poetry captured the imaginations of readers. She never saw her words celebrated or realized the impact her stark imagery had upon so many others. Her four simple words, "I dwell in possibility," reflect her belief that there are always steps one can take, always a path one can choose to follow.

Dickinson's incentive was *simplicity*, combined with a desire to express herself creatively.

Ralph Waldo Emerson, *Philosopher, essayist, lecturer, and literary critic, 1803–1882*

Here are two particularly thought-provoking quotes: "Make the most of yourself, for that is all there is of you," and "The reward of a thing well done is having done it." Both of these quotes speak to Emerson's view that it is important to get started and keep going, that nothing gets done unless you take that first step, and that there is gratification in the act of striving, as well as in accomplishment. (See page 88 for another Emerson quote.) Emerson applauded independence, intuition, nonconformity, reflection, and integrity. He was a doer—a leader, not a follower. He appreciated nature. He knew the importance of self-reliance and trusting oneself, and he wrote a great deal about this.

Emerson's incentive was *initiative*, combined with the strength of his convictions.

Don't underestimate the value of quotes or stories that you or your children already know and that convey worthwhile messages. These can stir up animated discussion. For example, take the age-old but very simple tale of the tortoise and the hare. This tale illustrates that deliberation and focus are good because slow and steady ultimately wins the race. The other side of the coin is that procrastinating and then rushing toward completion can lead to disappointment and failure. Two very useful complementary messages. Take a second look at this familiar fable with your child and frame it as a cautionary tale about procrastination.

Select another story about procrastination to read and discuss.[155] My all-time favorite book, suitable for anyone age six or older (and sure to be enjoyed by those who appreciate fun with words), is *The Phantom Tollbooth*, a delightful tale about a boy named Milo who always wastes time.[156] He embarks on a series of adventures in make-believe lands nestled between the Mountains of Ignorance and the Sea of Knowledge. He meets many strange but enlightening characters. Why not read a recreational book like this together, or tap into one studied in school and have a meaningful chat?[157] Look for song lyrics, movies, and television shows to provide a basis for stimulating thought and discussion.

Directions for Future Reference

I would like to close with this final thought, courtesy of Emily Dickinson: "Forever is composed of *nows*."[158]

Parents can push that agenda in the fervent hope that all the *nows* are productive. But the reality is that not all *nows* are equally productive.

Procrastination is not generally an "imminent danger" type of problem, but it can be debilitating and stressful for children. It can affect their initiative, achievement levels, relationships with others, happiness, and well-being. If your child is very distraught or you see changes in behavior that seem decidedly off, then, as mentioned before, it is time to consider consulting with a professional. There are trained clinicians who can help children and their parents deal with difficult and anxiety-provoking circumstances. A family doctor, psychologist, guidance counselor, or educational consultant can offer direction and support.

Parents can help their children become more productive, confident, and resolute by showing why perseverance matters and by adopting a growth mindset.[159] Adults who tend to procrastinate can also try some of these many suggestions, independently or alongside children so as to encourage each other. Effort and commitment can be empowering, and when kids see the adults in their lives working hard, learning, and being resilient, the message conveyed is very clear—there are ways to get things done! Share with your children some of the strategies you have read about in these pages to help them overcome procrastination. Demonstrate resourcefulness and initiative. Talk to them about your concerns so that you can work together to increase their productivity. Do it *now*.

References

Andeou, C., & White, M. D. (2012). *The thief of time: Philosophical essays on procrastination*. New York: Oxford University Press.

Barish, K. (2013, September 9). How do children learn to regulate their emotions?. *Huff Post Parents*. http://www.huffingtonpost.com/kenneth-barish-phd/how-do-children-learn-to-_b_3890461.html

Barlow, D. (2014). *Clinical handbook of psychological disorders, 5th edition*. New York: The Guilford Press.

Baycrest, (2012, October 13). *The virtual brain project*. http://www.baycrest.org/care/culture-arts-innovation/arts-science-technology/the-virtual-brain-project/

Beery, R., & Covington, M. (1976). *Self-worth and school learning*. New York: Holt, Rinehart & Winston.

Brown, M. (1947). *Stone soup*. New York: Simon and Shuster.

Burka, J. B., & Yuen, L. M. (2008). *Procrastination: Why you do it, what to do about it now*. Cambridge, MA: Da Capo Press.

Callard-Szulgit, R. (2012). *Perfectionism and gifted children, 2nd edition*. Lanham, MD: Rowman and Littlefield.

Carnegie, D. (2010). *How to win friends and influence people*. New York: Simon and Schuster.

Chua, A. (2011). *Hymn of the Tiger Mother*. New York: Penguin.

Covey, S. R. (2004). *The seven habits of highly effective people: Powerful lessons in personal change*. New York: Simon & Schuster.

Covey, S.R. (2014). *The seven habits of highly effective teens*. New York: Simon & Schuster.

Dell'Antonia, K. J. (2014, January 27). Age-appropriate chores for children (and why they're not doing them). *New York Times: Motherlode, Living the Family Dynamic.* http://parenting.blogs.nytimes.com/2014/01/27/age-appropriate-chores-for-children-and-why-theyre-not-doing-them/?_php=true&_type=blogs&_r=0

Dickens, C. (1838). *Oliver Twist.* London: Richard Bentley.

Dolan, P. (2014, August 29). Happiness is in the details. [Interview]. *Globe and Mail.*

Dolan, P. (2014). *Happiness by design: Change what you do, not how you think.* London: Hudson Street Press.

Dreikurs, R., & Soltz, V. (1991). *Children: The challenge.* New York: Plume.

Dweck, C. (2006). *Mindset: The new psychology of success.* New York: Ballantine Books.

Elliot, A. J., & Dweck, C. S. (2007). *Handbook of competence and motivation.* New York: Guilford Press.

Emmett, R. (2002). Quotes from *The procrastinating child: A handbook for adults to help children stop putting things off.* New York: Walker & Co. http://www.ritaemmett.com/book_child_quotes.htm

Erikson, E. H. (1993). *Childhood and society.* New York: W. W. Norton & Company.

Ferrari, J. R., Johnson, J. L., & McCown, W. G. (1995). *Procrastination and task avoidance: Theory, research and treatment.* New York: Springer.

Foster, J. F. (2007, December). Procrastination and perfectionism; Connections, understandings, and control. *Gifted Education International, 23,* 132-140. http://gei.sagepub.com/content/23/3/264.abstract

Foster, J. F. (2009). Intrinsic and extrinsic motivation. In B. A. Kerr (Ed.), *The encyclopedia of giftedness, creativity and talent,* p 490-491. New York: Sage.

Foster, J. F. (2013, January 3). *Children and change: Perspectives, implications, and strategies.* http://jffoster.wordpress.com/2013/01/03/children-and-change-perspectives-implications-and-strategies/

Foster, J. F. (2013, September 1). *Critical thinking skills: Essential for coping successfully with challenge and change.* http://jffoster.wordpress.com/2013/09/01/critical-thinking-skills-essential-for-coping-successfully-with-challenge-and-change/

Foster, J. F. (2013, September 7). *Challenge and effort: A mindset perspective.* http://jffoster.wordpress.com/2013/09/07/challenge-and-effort-a-mindset-perspective/

Foster, J. F. (2013, September 1). *Attunement and advocacy: Strengthening home and school connections.* http://jffoster.wordpress.com/2013/09/01/attunement-and-advocacy-strengthening-home-and-school-connections/

Foster, J. F. (2013, December). M is for motivation. *Parenting for High Potential.* Washington D.C.: National Association for Gifted Children.

Foster, J. F. (2014, July). P is for productivity. *Parenting for High Potential.* Washington D.C.: National Association for Gifted Children.

Foster, J. F. (2014, November 10). *A personal perspective on parents' praise.* Boomerang Health http://www.boomeranghealth.com/blog/psychology/personal-perspective-parents-praise/

Frank, A. (1993). *Anne Frank: The diary of a young girl.* New York: Bantam.

Gardner, H. (2011). *Frames of mind: The theory of multiple intelligences.* New York: Basic Books.

Gesner, C. (1985). Book Report. *You're a good man, Charlie Brown.* https://www.youtube.com/watch?v=HZEmxby8g8A

Gilman, B. (2008). *Academic advocacy for gifted children: A parent's complete guide.* Scottsdale, AZ: Great Potential Press.

Gilman, P. (1988). *Jillian Jiggs.* New York: Scholastic.

Gladwell, M. (2009). *Outliers: The story of success.* New York: Penguin.

Goleman, D. (2005). *Emotional intelligence: Why it can matter more than IQ.* New York: Bantam Books.

Gordon, T. (2011, January 17). Origins of the Gordon Model. *Gordon Training.* http://www.gordontraining.com/thomas-gordon/origins-of-the-gordon-model/

Greenspon, T. S. (2012). *Moving past perfect: How perfectionism may be holding back your kids (and you!) and what you can do about it.* Minneapolis, MN: Free Spirit.

Hallowell, E. M., & Ratey, J. J. (2005). *Delivered from distraction: Getting the most out of life with Attention Deficit Disorder.* New York: Random House.

Hallowell, E. M., & Ratey, J. J. (2011). *Driven to distraction: Recognizing and coping with Attention Deficit Disorder, revised.* New York: Ballantine Books.

Halsted, J. (2002). *Some of my best friends are books.* Scottsdale, AZ: Great Potential Press.

Heusen, J. V., & Cahn, S. (1959). *High hopes.* [Song].

Horowitz, F. D., Subotnik, R. F., & Matthews, D. J. (2009). *The development of giftedness and talent across the life span.* Washington, D.C.: American Psychological Association.

Hurley, K. (2013, March 6). 6 ways to help children cope with frustration. *Everyday Family.* http://www.everydayfamily.com/blog/6-ways-to-help-children-cope-with-frustration/

Johnson, J. A. (2012, November 30). Are 'I' statements better than 'you' statements? *Psychology Today.* http://www.psychologytoday.com/blog/cui-bono/201211/are-i-statements-better-you-statements

Juster, N. (1961). *The phantom tollbooth.* New York: Random House.

Kagan, J. (2010). *The temperamental thread: How genes, culture, time and luck make us who we are.* New York: Dana Press.

Kaufman, S. B. (2013). *Ungifted—Intelligence redefined: The truth about talent, practice, creativity, and the many paths to greatness.* New York: Basic Books.

Kerr, B. A. (2009). *The encyclopedia of giftedness, creativity, and talent.* New York: Sage.

Kids Now Canada. http://www.kidsnowcanada.org/

Kohn, A. (2014). *The myth of the spoiled child.* Cambridge, MA: Da Capo Press.

Knaus, W. (2010, June 18). Ten top tips to end writer's block procrastination. *Psychology Today.* http://www.psychologytoday.com/blog/science-and-sensibility/201006/ten-top-tips-end-writer-s-block-procrastination

Maraia, M. M. (2009). *Relationships are everything: Growing your business one relationship at a time.* Highlands Ranch, CO: Professional Services Publishing.

Matthews, D. (2013, July 25). *The four faces of "no": Finding the just-right sweet spot of parenting.* http://donamatthews.wordpress.com/2013/07/25/the-four-faces-of-no-finding-the-just-right-sweet-spot-of-parenting/

Matthews, D. (2014, November 5). *Overscheduled? Too busy to play? Six ways to push back and create a healthy balance for your kids.* http://beyondintelligence.net/2014/11/05/overscheduled-too-busy-to-play-six-ways-to-push-back-and-create-a-healthy-balance-for-your-kids/

Matthews, D. & Foster, J. F. (2009). *Being smart about gifted education, 2nd edition.* Scottsdale, AZ: Great Potential Press.

Matthews, D., & Foster, J. F. (2013, January 7). Mindsets and gifted education: Transformation in progress. *Growth Mindset Blog, Mindset Works.* http://community.mindsetworks.com/blog-page/home-blogs/entry/mindsets-and-gifted-education-transformation-in-progress

Matthews, D., & Foster, J. F. (2014). *Beyond intelligence: Secrets for raising happily productive kids.* Toronto, ON: House of Anansi Press.

Mindset Works. (2008). http://www.mindsetworks.com/

Mischel, W., Ebbesen, E. B., & Raskoff Zeiss, A. (1972, February). Cognitive and attentional mechanisms in delay of gratification. *Journal of Personality and Social Psychology, 21(2)*, 204-218.

Mitchell, M. (1936). *Gone with the wind.* New York: Scribner Book Company.

Munsch, R. (2004). *Smelly socks.* Toronto, ON: Scholastic Canada.

Nair, A. (2013, November 12). *Tips for ending homework stress.* http://www.yummymumyclub.ca/blogs/andrea-nair-button-pushing/20131111/tips-for-ending-homework-stress.

Neihart, M. (2008). *Peak performance for smart kids.* Waco, TX: Prufrock Press.

Olszewski-Kubilius, P. (2013, June). Swimming in bigger ponds. *Parenting for High Potential*, pp. 2, 3, 16. Washington D.C.: National Association for Gifted Children.

Peters, D. (2013). *Make your worrier a warrior.* Tucson, AZ: Great Potential Press.

Popova, M. (2012, September 21). The science of procrastination and how to manage it, animated. *Brain Pickings.* http://www.brainpickings.org/index.php/2012/09/21/the-science-of-procrastination/

Porge, S. W. (1995). Orienting a defensive world: Mammalian modifications of our evolutionary heritage: A polyvagal theory. *Psychophysiology, 32*, 301-308.

Portnoy, F. (2012). *Wait: The art and science of delay.* New York: Perseus Book Group.

Price-Mitchell, M. (2013). What is a role model? Five qualities that matter to teens. *Roots of Action.* http://www.rootsofaction.com/what-is-a-role-model-five-qualities-that-matter-for-role-models/ Retrieved Nov. 20, 2014.

Price-Mitchell, M. (2013). How role models influence youth strategies for success. *Roots of Action* http://www.rootsofaction.com/role-models-youth-strategies-success/ Retrieved Nov. 20, 2014.

Procrasti-Nation. (2008). *Slate.* http://www.slate.com/articles/life/procrastination/2008/05/procrastination.html

Procrastination—The Musical. (2012, December 4). https://www.youtube.com/watch?v=Xi3aEGo8y-E

Procrastination Research Group. (2001). Carleton University, Ottawa, Canada, Department of Psychology. http://http-server.carleton.ca/~tpychyl/

Pychyl, T. (2013). *Solving the procrastination puzzle: A concise guide to strategies for change.* New York: Tarcher.

Radcliffe, S. C. (2013). *The fear fix: Solutions for every child's moments of worry, panic, and fear.* Toronto, ON: HarperCollins.

Renzulli, J. (1977). *Interest-A-Lyzer.* Mansfield Center, CT: Creative Learning Press.

Rimm, S. (2008). *Why bright kids get poor grades: And what you can do about it, 3rd edition.* Scottsdale, AZ: Great Potential Press.

Rivero, L. (2010). *A parent's guide to gifted teens.* Scottsdale, AZ: Great Potential Press.

Rivero, L. (2014, August 14). *Breaking free from procrastination.* http://www.lisarivero.com/2014/08/14/procrastination/

Rogers, K. B. (2002). *Re-forming gifted education: How parents and teachers can match the program to the child.* Scottsdale, AZ: Great Potential Press.

Ruf, D. (2009.) *Talent Igniter.* http://www.talentigniter.com/

Sapadin, L., & Maguire, J. (1998). *How to beat procrastination and make the grade.* New York: Penguin.

Schafer, A. (2007, December 2). *Getting kids to school on time.* http://alysonschafer.com/getting-kids-to-school-on-time/

Schafer, A. (2009). *Ain't misbehavin'.* Toronto: Harper Collins.

Seligman, M. (1975). *Helplessness: On depression, development, and death.* San Francisco: W.H. Freeman.

Shanker, S. (2010). Self regulation and learning. *TEDx YMCA Academy.* https://www.youtube.com/watch?v=HTbAFmOdImY

Shanker, S. (2012). *Calm, alert and learning: Classroom strategies for self-regulation.* Toronto: ON. Pearson Education, Canada.

Shanker, S. (2014, April 10). Why are Canadian kids so stressed out?. *Huff Post Living Canada.* http://www.huffingtonpost.ca/stuart-shanker/kids-stress-canada_b_5120663.html

Shaughnessy, M. (2010). An interview with Dona Matthews and Joanne Foster about teaching gifted students higher order and critical thinking skills. *The International Journal of Creativity and Problem Solving, 20(1),* 73-79.

Steel, P. (2007). The nature of procrastination: A meta-analytic and theoretical review of quintessential self-regulatory failure. *Psychological Bulletin, 133(1),* 65–94.

Taylor, J. (2010, September 27). Parenting: Frustration in children: Aarrgghh!. *Psychology Today.* http://www.psychologytoday.com/blog/the-power-prime/201009/parenting-frustration-in-children-aarrgghh

Too Small to Fail. http://toosmall.org/ or https://www.clintonfoundation.org/our-work/too-small-fail

Tough, P. (2012). *How children succeed: Grit, curiosity, and the hidden power of character.* Boston, MA: Mariner Books.

Vaden, R. (2012). *Take the stairs: 7 Steps to achieving true success*. New York: Penguin.

Van Tassel-Baska, J., & Stambaugh, T. (2006). *Comprehensive curriculum for gifted learners, 3rd edition*. New York: Pearson.

Vygotsky, L. S. (1978). *Mind in society: The development of higher psychological processes*. Cambridge, MA: Harvard University Press.

Webb, J., Gore, J., Amend, E., & Devries, A. (2007). *A parent's guide to gifted children*. Scottsdale, AZ. Great Potential Press.

Wells, K. (2014). Documentary: How does your engine run?. *The Sunday Edition with Michael Enright*. CBC Radio.

Whitney, C. S., & Hirsch, G. (2007). *A love for learning: Motivation and the gifted child*. Scottsdale, AZ: Great Potential Press.

Willis, J. (2008). *Inspiring middle school minds*. Scottsdale, AZ: Great Potential Press.

Wohl, M. J. A., Pychyl, T. A., & Bennett, S. H. (2010). I forgive myself, now I can study: How self-forgiveness for procrastinating can reduce future procrastination. *Personality and Individual Differences, 48*, 803–808.

Woolfolk, A. E., Winne, P. H., & Perry, N. E. (2012). *Educational Psychology, 5th* Ed. Toronto, ON: Pearson Canada.

Endnotes

Introduction

1   In *Being Smart about Gifted Education*, 2009, Dona Matthews and Joanne Foster explore ways to support and encourage children's high-level development.
2   Foster, 2007.

Chapter 1

3   Educators and psychologists often refer to this as a lack of self-efficacy.
4   Strategies are provided for many of these reasons, and readers will find these quite readily by checking the index for specific topics, or by looking in the table of contents for headings that will pinpoint the applicable section.
5   Ferrari, Johnson, & McCown, 1995, p. 11 & p. 28.
6   In *Hymn of the Tiger Mother*, author Amy Chua discusses the strict approach she used while raising her own children. This book has generated considerable controversy. In the end, parents have to choose child-rearing practices that they feel work best for them.
7   Burka & Yuen, 2008, p. 6.
8   Rivero, 2010, p.123.
9   Lisa Rivero describes such struggles in her blog post "Breaking Free from Procrastination" (http://www.lisarivero.com/2014/08/14/procrastination/).

Chapter 2

10   Common sense, good judgment, decision making, and self regulation are all skills that children acquire as they mature. These skills have to do with executive functioning.
11   Names have been changed throughout this book to protect privacy.
12   Each of these topics as related to procrastination is discussed elsewhere in this book. Overload is a key aspect of Chapter 7. A chunk of Chapter 3 is devoted to helping kids deal with avoidance behavior as relating to stress. Boredom and lack of motivation, and difficulties with schoolwork are addressed in various spots, including Chapter 6 and part of Chapter 11.

13   When procrastination presents as belligerent or aggressive behavior, it may indicate an underlying issue that could be attitudinal or have risen a head of steam. Sometimes children need help learning how to vent their frustrations (or worries, or anger, or other emotions) in healthy and more productive ways. Much has been written on this subject. Links to three articles with practical advice for parents follow here:
     http://www.psychologytoday.com/blog/the-power-prime/201009/
          parenting-frustration-in-children-aarrgghh
     http://www.everydayfamily.com/blog/6-ways-to-help-children-cope-with-
          frustration/
     http://www.huffingtonpost.com/kenneth-barish-phd/how-do-children-
          learn-to-_b_3890461.html.

14   Mitchell, 1936.

15   From *The Diary of Anne Frank* and displayed on a memorial plaque in the house where she was hidden for years during the war, now the Anne Frank Museum in Amsterdam.

16   Brown, 1947. The tale *Stone Soup* was written by Marcia Brown and won a Caldecott Award. Since then the story has appeared in various adaptations by different authors.

17   From *You're a Good Man Charlie Brown* – "The Book Report" – animated version retrieved from http://www.youtube.com/watch?v=HZEmxby8g8A.

18   Sapadin & Maguire, 1998. A few of these personas have been inspired by a book by Linda Sapadin and Jack Maguire. There, and in more recent work by Sapadin, the writing revolves around six specific "styles of procrastinators"—perfectionist, overdoer, dreamer, worrier, crisis-maker, and defier. That approach is organized and interesting; however, I have differentiated and greatly extended the range here, and I don't rely on these kinds of categorical descriptors elsewhere in my book.

19   An excellent book on the subject of emotional intelligence is Daniel Goleman's *Emotional Intelligence: Why It Can Matter More Than IQ*, 2005.

20   A nod to the Charles Dickens character the Artful Dodger in *Oliver Twist*.

Chapter 3

21   Vygotsky, 1978. Self-talk is a process whereby people use words or thoughts to guide them through a task. Developmental psychologist Lev Vygotsky wrote about how children often narrate their actions aloud, and then, eventually, silently. He referred to this as inner speech. Adults sometimes engage in this process as well.

22   Dweck, 2006.

23   Dweck, 2009, p. xii.

24   Beery & Covington, 1976.

25   Dweck, 2006, p. 21.

26   For more on learned helplessness, see *Being Smart about Gifted Education* by Matthews, D. & Foster, J., 2009. For original studies on learned helplessness, see the work by Seligman, M., *Helplessness: On Depression, Development, and Death*, 1975.

27 Matthews & Foster, 2013, January 7.

28 Webb, Gore, Amend, & Devries, 2007.

29 With respect to the phobias being illogical, for example, it is unlikely that a centipede sitting in a bathtub is going to attack a human. Yet there are plenty of people who won't go anywhere near it without a heavy-soled shoe in one shaking hand and a can of seriously potent bug spray in the other—and that's only if they can't find someone else to get rid of it. They can't simply ignore the creepy crawling thing because it will be lurking.

30 Barlow, 2014.

31 Resources to consult include *Make your Worrier a Warrior* by Dan Peters, 2013, which guides parents and teachers in "taming the worry monster" and also *The Fear Fix: Solutions for Every Child's Moments of Worry, Panic, and Fear* by Sarah Chana Radcliffe, 2014.

32 For additional relaxation methods, including tapping, focusing techniques, aromatherapy, and more, see *The Fear Fix: Solutions for Every Child's Moments of Worry, Panic, and Fear* by Sarah Chana Radcliffe, 2013.

33 Online possibilities to explore include the Breathe2Relax app; Inner Balance app (by HeartMath) and Magic Eye focusing images.

34 Many professional support organizations provide resources, practitioners, and up-to-date information on therapies and clinical options for dealing with phobias and stress. Reputable frontline institutions can be found across the globe, online, and within communities that are close to home and accessible when the need arises. Their mission is to help parents as they work to address children's mental health and other issues. As a starting point, additional information can be found at http://www.nimh.nih.gov/index.shtml.

35 Dona Matthews has written an excellent piece offering parents six strategies to help kids who experience too much "busyness" and not enough balance in their lives. http://beyondintelligence.net/2014/11/05/overscheduled-too-busy-to-play-six-ways-to-push-back-and-create-a-healthy-balance-for-your-kids/.

36 HALT is an acronym for a program that embraces the principle of attending to one's primary needs—hunger, anger, loneliness, and tiredness. This is sound advice, shared by many counselors and treatment organizations online and elsewhere.

37 Shanker, 2012.

38 For information about issues related to ADHD, see books by Edward M. Hallowell and John J. Ratey, *Driven to Distraction (Revised): Recognizing and Coping with Attention Deficit Disorder*, 2011, and also *Delivered from Distraction: Getting the Most out of Life with Attention Deficit Disorder*, 2005.

39 This technique of praising the behavior you want to occur beforehand is described in *A Parent's Guide to Gifted Children*, by Webb et al., 2007.

40 Stuart Shanker provides information to help children regulate their emotions (including identifying feelings and learning how to become calmer). See http://

www.huffingtonpost.ca/stuart-shanker/kids-stress-canada_b_5120663.html
and also www.youtube.com/watch?v=HTbAFmOdImY.

41   This was said by Martin Luther, and later by Martin Luther King.

Chapter 4

42   Dr. Seuss quote—retrieved on Nov. 28th 2014 at http://www.brainyquote.
com/quotes/authors/d/dr_seuss.html. And, just for fun, here's another
quote: "*You have brains in your head, you have feet in your shoes. You can
steer yourself in any direction you choose.*"

43   For tips on how to praise children so as to encourage their intelligence,
creativity, and productivity, see *A Personal Perspective on Parents' Praise*,
posted by Boomerang Health, part of the Sick Children's Hospital Network in Toronto at http://www.boomeranghealth.com/blog/psychology/
personal-perspective-parents-praise/.

44   The psychologist Thomas Gordon emphasizes that it is more helpful
to use *I-statements* rather than to blame the child saying *You*. Though
this technique is fairly widely known, you can find more information at
http://www.gordontraining.com/thomas-gordon/origins-of-the-gordon-
model/ and http://www.psychologytoday.com/blog/cui-bono/201211/
are-i-statements-better-you-statements.

45   Sometimes these social and cultural influences emphasize procrastination
as a major flaw; others are more tolerant and lenient. Nonetheless, adults
need to be alert to procrastination so that it does not become an entrenched
behavior that handicaps the child's ability to achieve and to relate to others.

46   Dreikurs & Soltz, 1991. Rudolph Dreikurs and Vicki Soltz, in their classic
child-rearing book *Children: The Challenge,* do an excellent job of describing how parents can implement natural and logical consequences to help
children learn self-management skills.

47   Power struggles can happen with older children as well. The topic of power
struggles is addressed more fully in Chapter 9.

48   To find out more about Erik Erikson (1902-1994) and his psychosocial
theory of personal development see his book, *Childhood and Society*, 1993.

49   Foster, 2013, September 1.

50   Involvement is good, but endless hovering or hyper-involvement can be
counterproductive. Things tend to work best in moderation.

51   Rita Emmett's acronym-based strategies for children http://www.ritaemmett.
com/book_child_quotes.htm.

52   William Knaus raises this particular point (in an article about writer's block).
He notes that "*Can't* implies that an action is outside of your capability… *Won't*
thinking is a reason for optimism because this thinking is changeable." Knaus
also discusses the importance of being decisive—that is, setting a workable
time frame, creating a plan of action, and staying committed to it.
http://www.psychologytoday.com/blog/science-and-sensibility/201006/
ten-top-tips-end-writer-s-block-procrastination.

53   For more on advocacy, see Attunement and Advocacy: Strengthening Home and School Connections, http://jffoster.wordpress.com/?s=Strengthening+ Home+and+School+Connections. Additional material on advocacy and parental involvement in schools is accessible at www.beyondintelligence.net.

54   Message conveyed by actress Cate Blanchett on *60 Minutes*, Feb. 16th, 2014— when discussing that what she's found most challenging or complicated about her many accomplishments is just "beginning."

Chapter 5

55   See endnote 51 regarding resources on advocacy, and refer also to *Being Smart about Gifted Education*, 2nd Ed. by Dona Matthews and Joanne Foster, 2009.

56   See Foster's "Intrinsic and Extrinsic Motivation", pp. 490-491 from *The Encyclopedia of Giftedness, Creativity and Talent* edited by Barbara Kerr, 2009, and also Foster's "M is for Motivation," which was published in NAGC's *Parenting for High Potential*, (Winter 2014). Both resources are readily accessible at www.beyondintelligence.net. Two other useful resources: Elliot & Dweck's *Handbook of Competence and Motivation*, 2007, and Whitney & Hirsch's *Love for Learning: Motivation and the Gifted Child*, 2007.

57   Some developmental changes may appear suddenly or abruptly, like a growth spurt, but these are actually preceded by smaller and often unseen changes. Learning by leaps and bounds—like gaining the ability to elaborate on stories, understand complex mathematical equations, or operate a sailboat—doesn't happen overnight, but rather over time and with experience. Whether it has to do with literacy, numeracy, motor skills, social competence, or other capacities, children progress from the simple, grasping basic schemes, through to the composite, merging and synchronizing what they know and can do. All of this requires involvement and understandings about the domain, whether it is literature, geometry, seafaring, or something else altogether. With instruction, effort, and practice, ultimately, this leads to being able to master complexities as well as being able to apply accumulated knowledge to different kinds of activities and problems.

58   Walter, Ebbesen, & Raskoff Zeiss, 1972.

59   http://en.wikipedia.org/wiki/Stanford_marshmallow_experiment. For those who want to find out more about this gratification research, there are many online sources and even several "marshmallow study" videos online.

60   Covey, 1989.

61   See Posner in *Procrasti-Nation*, an article by Slate, 2008, with comments by various people in America who procrastinate (http://www.slate.com/ articles/life/procrastination/2008/05/procrastination.html).

62   Resources include Carol Dweck's *Mindset*, 2006, and Rory Vaden's *Take the Stairs: 7 Steps to Achieving True Success*, 2012; for those who want to dabble in philosophy, consider relaying and chatting about the messages in *The Thief of Time: Philosophical Essays on Procrastination* by Chisoula Andeou and Mark D. White, 2012.

63   See *Children: The Challenge* by Dreikurs and Soltz regarding natural consequences. Also worth noting here is the Montessori approach with its focus
on independence and structure.

64   See Vygotsky on private speech in *Educational Psychology,* 5th edition, by
Woolfolk, Winne, and Perry, 2012, pp. 43-45.

65   Tough, 2012.

66   Chinese proverb.

67   Vaden, 2012. Everyone wastes time. It's true! Rory Vaden states that in a
study of 10,000 employees in the US, the average worker admitted to 2.09
wasted hours daily. That is, time spent on activities that weren't job related.
If adults are guilty of wasting time, is it any surprise that kids are, too?

68   Information about identity as noted in *Educational Psychology* by Woolfolk,
Winne, & Perry, 2009, p. 89.

69   Developmental psychologist James Marcia builds on Erikson's work and
says that teenagers can experience one or more of four different identity
alternatives. According to Marcia, *identity diffusion* refers to adolescent role
confusion, in which teens don't explore options or commit to actions. They
lack direction and may seem apathetic or withdrawn. *Identity foreclosure*
is about commitment without exploration—teens adhere to and adopt the
goals and values of family members or others, but not as a result of their own
searching. *Identity moratorium* is a term that refers to a gradual process, as
a teenager develops an ideology or sense of self. Sometimes this occurs with
struggle, and sometimes with suspending choices or delaying action along
the way. *Identity achievement* also takes time, often extending beyond the
high school years. A person who has reached this fourth state has arrived at
a point of commitment and can confidently answer the question "Who am
I?" after having carefully considered alternatives and having made decisions
leading up to that point. Of course, this does not preclude further changes
about the self down the road, with even more maturity. These four identity
states are interesting from a procrastination standpoint because they help
to position where a teen might be in relation to personal explorations and
commitments and this, in turn, can have a bearing on productivity. However, as a cautionary note, these identity status descriptors are not meant
to be diagnostic in relation to any one particular child.

70   Throughout this book I emphasize the importance of role models. Marilyn
Price-Mitchell wrote an informative article describing the top five
qualities of effective role models—people who inspire "young people
to develop the skills, abilities, and motivation to become engaged citi-
zens." The qualities include passion and ability to inspire, a clear set of
values, commitment to community, selflessness and acceptance of others,
and the ability to overcome obstacles (http://www.rootsofaction.com/
what-is-a-role-model-five-qualities-that-matter-for-role-models/).

    In a follow-up piece, she explains how and why role models are
instrumental as kids develop behaviors, aspirations, and educational goals. She asks, "Who do kids emulate?" She talks about the

importance of a growth mindset and describes how to help kids bring other positive role models into their lives (http://www.rootsofaction.com/role-models-youth-strategies-success/).

71   Some of us function better at night, others in the morning, adhering to our individual Circadian rhythms. Some function better at definite times of the month due to hormonal rhythm, and during puberty, that rhythm tends to be erratic. There are those who work better at certain times of the year, based on the amount of sunlight and darkness, based on a seasonal rhythm. Our personal biological states are unique, and vary like the ebb and flow of the tides.

72   *The Seven Habits of Highly Effective Teens* by Sean Covey, 1998, is interesting reading for adolescents who struggle with procrastination. The author suggests that the seven habits can help teenagers improve relationships with parents and friends; make smarter decisions; overcome addiction; increase self-confidence; feel happier; get more done in less time; define personal values and what matters most; and balance various aspects of life. *The Seven Habits of Highly Effective People: Powerful Lessons in Personal Change*, another book by Covey, focuses on similar themes.

73   Colleges typically provide links and resources to information sites designed to help kids with planning. There are also privately run places across North America for people who want to pay for guidance around post secondary-school decision making.

74   For more about helping kids prepare for college and other post-secondary school options, see *Beyond Intelligence: Secrets for Raising Happily Productive Kids* by Dona Matthews and Joanne Foster, 2014, pp. 80-85.

Chapter 6

75   Deborah Ruf, a psychologist who works in the field of high-level development, has created an interesting planning tool, called the *Talent Igniter*. This is an example of an appoach parents can investigate further. http://www.talentigniter.com.

76   There are many different kinds of assessments to determine the nature of your child's needs, along with instructional ideas to meet those needs. Some of these assessments are formal and must be administered by specifically trained professionals, others can be administered by classroom teachers; some are individual and others are group-oriented; still others are informal and readily accessible online. Examples of informal assessments that parents can refer to in order to determine a child's areas of strength and weakness, interests, and learning preferences include Howard Gardner's Multiple Intelligences Inventory, Joseph Renzulli's Interest-A-Lyser, and Karen Rogers' frameworks for assessing learning needs in her book, *Re-Forming Gifted Education: How Parents and Teachers Can Match the Program to the Child.*

77   In *Being Smart about Gifted Education*, Dona Matthews and I discuss the who, what, where, when, why, and how of testing and identification

procedures. The information we provide is applicable to learners functioning at various levels of capability. We explain why people should be cautious about tests and testing, including individual and group-administered IQ tests, and we express some concern that inaccurate information about a child's abilities can be generated and communicated to parents and others in the throes of making programming and placement decisions. The concern bears serious consideration because of the long-term implications for a child's self-esteem and subsequent academic achievement, as well as future decision-making processes. For more information see Section II of *Being Smart about Gifted Education, 2nd Edition*, 2009.

78   ADHD (Attention Deficit Hyperactivity Disorder) is one fairly common diagnosis among children who have difficulty focusing, shifting gears from one task to another or multitasking. There is a great deal of reference material pertaining to ADHD. I think one of the best resources is *Driven to Distraction* by Hallowell & Ratey, 2011.

79   There are many different kinds of assessments. Some are administered individually, and others are group-oriented. However, a word of caution. Although tests can provide valuable information about a child's areas of strength and weakness, even the most valid and reliable tests can yield low scores for reasons that are quite separate from ability. For example, a student may perform poorly on a test of cognitive ability because of distractions, lack of motivation, poor health, fatigue, anxiety—and these are just some considerations. Parents also have to recognize that such tests don't measure everything that matters in life, including values, tenacity, well-being, creativity, and more. Plus, children develop at different rates, and tests may not capture capactites that aren't yet realized. So when considering any kind of assessment of children's cognitive capabilites in relation to concerns, it is important to remember that these tests are not infallible measures of what someone can do, nor are they predictors of future success. Parents should take time to reflect upon the multiple day-to-day indicators of how their child is functioning, indicators such as learning portfolios, teachers' daily assessments, and a thoughtful review of the various experiences and factors that contribute to productive learning outcomes and overall well-being.

80   At the National Association for Gifted Children Conference (November 4, 2011), Del Siegle spoke about self-efficacy. He discussed the importance of skills, meaningfulness (fixing goal valuation into a task), and a supportive environment (with realistic expectations and appropriate strategies so children can complete goals and attain success). He also indicated that females tend to have lower self-efficacy than males, whereas males have lower self-regulation than females. Parents may want to investigate Siegle's work further.

81   "Reinforcing efforts and persistence, and helping students to cultivate a growth mindset about the nature of intelligence—that is, understanding it as being incremental and not fixed—are other ways to increase intrinsic

motivation." –Joanne Foster from "Intrinsic and Extrinsic Motivation" in *Encyclopedia of Giftedness, Creativity, and Talent,* by Barbara Kerr, 2009.

82 The website www.procrastination.ca from the University of Carleton, in Ottawa, Canada, has research information related to task avoidance and procrastination. There are lots of articles, strategies, and ideas for addressing the void that sometimes occurs between a person's intentions and actions.

83 Readers can check out "P is for Productivity" in the July 2014 issue of *Parenting for High Potential,* published by the National Association for Gifted Children. (The article is part of "ABCs of Being Smart" a series of featured columns that I write for the journal.) This particular piece focuses on planning and preparation; proper programming; play; paying attention; possible problems; and practice and persistence. There are also practical pointers to help kids overcome perfectionism and procrastination. The article is posted (along with others in the series) on the resources page at www.beyondintelligence.net.

84 Matthews & Foster, 2009.

85 Gladwell, 2009.

86 Emerson quote, retrieved December, 2014 at http://www.brainyquote.com/quotes/authors/r/ralph_waldo_emerson_2.html#yeIJ2TQvSmQdELIE.99.

87 Paula Olsziewski-Kubilius writes about the effects of "swimming in bigger ponds" in an article with that title in the June 2013 issue of *Parenting for High Potential,* a journal published by the National Association for Gifted Children. She discusses some of the issues that come to the fore when children move from one academic and social context to another that is more advanced or competitive, and what parents can do to help ease the transition process and foster children's perceptions of their abilities.

88 For more tips on advocacy, see *Being Smart about Gifted Education* by Matthews and Foster, 2009, and *Academic Advocacy for Gifted Children: A Parent's Complete Guide* by Barbara Gilman, 2008.

89 Foster, 2013, September 1.

90 For more information on different issues that can arise in relation to parenting and educating gifted learners, and for a wide range of gifted resources and links, including online sources, newsletters, books, and publishers, go to http://beyondintelligence.net.

Chapter 7

91 Peters, 2013.

92 Thomas Greenspon, a psychologist, wrote *Moving Past Perfect: How Perfectionism May Be Holding Back Your Kids (and You!) and What You Can Do About It,* 2012. He discusses what it means to strive for excellence—which can lead to high achievement—as opposed to being perfectionistic—which can be debilitating and inhibit performance. Greenspon provides information about the nature of perfectionism. He also discusses the importance of thinking carefully about praise, encouragement, anger, acceptance, aspirations, stress, and more. These topics have a direct bearing on children's

productivity and well-being. Greenspon uses illustrative stories as spring-boards for thought, and offers activities and strategies to help children overcome perfectionism.

93   Steel, 2007.

94   One can read further about the theory that perfectionism leads to procras-tination online and in peer-reviewed journals. Authors and researchers who have written about this include Kristie L. Speirs Neumeister, Michael Pyryt, Sal Mendaglio, and Linda Silverman.

95   *High Hopes* was first popularized by Frank Sinatra, with music written by Jimmy Van Heusen and lyrics by Sammy Cahn. It was introduced in the 1959 film *A Hole in the Head*. The song was nominated for a Grammy and won an Oscar for Best Original Song at the 32nd Academy Awards.

96   These ideas and more are discussed in an interview with Paul Dolan entitled "Happiness is in the Details," published in the *Globe and Mail* on August 29, 2014. Dolan's book is entitled *Happiness by Design: Change What You Do, Not How You Think*.

97   For more information about mindfulness, including its benefits, go to www.discovermindfulness.ca.

98   Pychyl, 2013.

99   Wohl, Phychyl, & Bennett, 2010. Researcher Michael Wohl and his associates at Carleton University discovered that students who forgave themselves for procrastinating on studying for an exam procrastinated less on the next one.

100   Paraphrased from a quote by author Judith M. Knowlton, found at http://www.goodreads.com/quotes/27360-i-discovered-i-always-have-choices-and-sometimes-it-s-only.

101   Basic information on the ABCDE model is outlined through the American Institute for Preventive Medicine's Systematic Stress Management website at http://aipm.wellnesscheckpoint.com/library/banner_main.asp?P=1D88B5ASM56&zsection=ABCDE%20Model&lang=E&title=N. For a helpful summary of this model of self-talk, see pages 148-149 of *A Parents' Guide to Gifted Children*, by Webb et al. In this book, the authors refer to the "alphabet of resilience" and deviate slightly with the letters A and E, which they refer to as "adversity" (experiencing stressful events) and "energizing" (taking action after disputing beliefs and learning from that experience).

102   A special shout out and thank you to Camille Holzman for telling me about the *Procrastination—The Musical* online video clip.

Chapter 8

103   Sidney Crosby is a famous NHL hockey player. He was also the captain of the Canadian Olympic hockey team that won the gold medal at the recent 2014 games.

104   Van Tassel-Baska & Stambaugh, 2006.

105   Scott Barry Kaufman has also wrestled with the word *potential* (p. xvii). He is a psychologist, researcher, and author of *Ungifted—Intelligence Redefined:*

The Truth about Talent, Practice, Creativity, and the Many Paths to Greatness. Yet he struggled in grade school. He asks what counts. "Must you do well on standardized tests to achieve in life?" and "Where do roadblocks fit in?" (p. xx). (Which leads me to similarly wonder: Must you complete tests quickly? Can some challenges or tasks be left to simmer?) Kaufman reminds us, "Everyone has unique needs and is worthy of encouragement. In the real world, people clearly differ in their inclinations, passions, dreams, and goals" (p. xx). Wise counsel for parents of procrastinators. (In fact, wise counsel for everyone.)

106 Bill Gates, spoken on *60 Minutes*, aired July 28th, 2013.

107 Vygotsky, 1978. This is sometimes called the zone of proximal development. To find out more, check out work by Lev Vygotsky.

108 Deborah Ruf's *Talentigniter* at www.talentigniter.com.

109 Dweck, 2006; Vaden, 2012. For those who want to dabble in philosophy, consider relaying and chatting about the messages in *The Thief of Time: Philosophical Essays on Procrastination* by Chisoula Andeou and Mark D. White.

110 Rimm, 2008, p. 147.

111 Callard-Szulgit, 2012, p. 14.

112 Rimm, 2008, p. 148-151. Psychologist Sylvia Rimm writes that competitive experiences can gradually prepare kids for the different kinds of win/lose situations that will be inevitable as they get older. The world is a competitive place. Adults can help kids know that loss need not be threatening. Parents can emphasize children's improvements and personal bests, discuss how always coming in first is unrealistic, and show them how to record their own progress so they can appreciate their capabilities. This kind of thinking enables kids to think positively, confidently, and productively, rather than feeling pressured or defeated, and thereby helps them to stay engaged.

113 Foster, 2013, January, 3, http://jffoster.wordpress.com/2013/01/03/children-and-change-perspectives-implications-and-strategies/; Foster, 2013, September, 1, http://jffoster.wordpress.com/2013/09/01/critical-thinking-skills-essential-for-coping-successfully-with-challenge-and-change/.

114 Quote attributed to William G.T. Shedd, theologian, teacher, and pastor.

115 Here is an example: "I had confidence today. I learned from my mistakes and my experience, and I pulled it all together." These words were spoken by golfer Jason Dufner upon reflecting on winning his first PGA championship after many years on the circuit, on the Sports Channel, August 11, 2013.

Chapter 9

116 For more on Jerome Kagan's research, see *The Temperamental Thread: How Genes, Culture, Time and Luck Make Us Who We Are*, 2010.

117 For an interesting video on Stuart Shanker's Calm, Alert and Ready to Learn program, see *How Does Your Engine Run?* http://www.cbc.ca/news/how-does-your-engine-run-documentary-1.2445082.

118   The popular rhyming children's story *Jillian Jiggs* by Phoebe Gilman, 1988, is about a little girl who promises she will clean up her room. However, she is easily distracted by activities that are much more fun, and so she has difficulty getting the cleanup done. The book is geared for the younger set (ages three to six) but it is a delightful read at any age (http://www.goodreads.com/book/show/201041.Jillian_Jiggs).

119   Dell'Antonia, 2014, http://parenting.blogs.nytimes.com/2014/01/27/age-appropriate-chores-for-children-and-why-theyre-not-doing-them/?_php=true&_type=blogs&_r=0.

120   Alyson Schafer shares interesting perspectives about strategies and consequences in relation to getting dawdling kids to school in the morning (http://alysonschafer.com/getting-kids-to-school-on-time/).

121   In their classic book *Children: The Challenge*, Rudolph Dreikurs and Vicki Soltz describe the importance of family meetings as well as how to establish them as a family tradition.

122   Points listed under "looming large" (in Chapter 1) may also be applicable for coping with long-term assignments.

123   Author and psychotherapist Andrea Nair writes, "To preserve the love of learning, it is really important that homework keeps up with the times… and fosters development, not resistance." She offers suggestions for working with a child's teachers to "decrease homework issues" and "keep the focus on useful, not busy-work homework." She also provides resources for those with homework concerns. See http://www.yummymumyclub.ca/blogs/andrea-nair-button-pushing/20131111/tips-for-ending-homework-stress.

Chapter 10

124   Willis, 2008.

125   Porge, 1995. Scientists are investigating the science of delay through the neurological aspects and the connection to emotional health. Stephen Porge has done some work that deals with children's responses to stimuli. What happens physiologically when a child freezes in panic? Or when he is alert and ready to face a challenge? In his work, Porge looks at heart rate variability in the face of challenge. In short, he notes that there are differences in how the heart responds, showing a relationship between emotional experiences and heart regulation. His polyvagal theory focuses on the 10th cranial nerve (called the vagal or vagus) which consists of multiple strands that carry signals throughout our bodies. Porge refers to the "old reptilian" aspect of the vagus and the "new mammalian" aspect (think tortoise and hare). Where reptiles move slowly in steady but rather underpowered fashion, mammals can move in a "supercharged" way for short but invigorated periods of time. People are capable of both of these responses.

126   Dan Peters describes many techniques in *Make Your Worrier a Warrior*, 2013.

127   For additional information, see Maureen Neihart's *Peak Performance for Smart Kids*, 2008, p. 99-105.

128 For more on this, see Burka and Yuen's *Procrastination: Why You Do It, What to Do about it Now*, 2008, p. 102-103.

129 Portnoy, 2012, p. 267.

130 More information about the virtual brain can be found at http://www. baycrest.org/care/culture-arts-innovation/arts-science-technology/the-virtual-brain-project/#sthash.2FSz7lDM.dpuf.

131 In particular, children can learn about how the brain has the capacity to change—it develops and reorganizes itself in response to experience. This "plasticity" can generate new and adaptive behavior so no one needs to be stuck in any one behavioral pattern.

132 For more information about *Brainology*, go to www.mindsetworks.com.

133 A program funded in part by the Clinton Foundation is "Too Small to Fail" and it emphasizes the importance of reading to children from the earliest days. For more information go to www.toosmall.org, or to find out about and get involved in other programs designed to improve the lives of children visit https://www.clintonfoundation.org/our-work/too-small-fail.

134 A short animated video clip with a scientific approach to managing procrastination can be seen online at http://www.brainpickings.org/index. php/2012/09/21/the-science-of-procrastination/. In addition to a brief discussion about temporal discounting, the video offers suggestions for time management including offering rewards at intervals, removing distractions, helping kids set self-imposed costly deadlines as inducements for action, and reinforcing the joy of productivity.

135 Neihart, 2008, pp. 73-74.

136 Oliver, the student in Miss Gilroy's class who was very capable but had a heavy workload, decided to put off his math assignment. He may have been procrastinating but he was also strengthening his ability to prioritize demands, and learning to pace himself in a manner that best suited him.

137 Kids Now is an excellent example of an extracurricular skills development program. It is offered to middle school students in approximately 200 schools across Canada. With a focus on topics such as goal-setting, conflict resolution, communication and relationship-building, self-confidence, and stress management, students in grades 7 and 8 learn strategies for use at home and school. http://www.kidsnowcanada.org.

Chapter 11

138 Neihart, 2008, p. 166.

139 Actually it was a gym—located in the lower level of Branksome Hall, an independent girls' school in Toronto—with banners and all the rest, but with real seats as opposed to bleachers. This particular presentation took place in 2012.

140 This material is extracted from Joanne Foster's blog post titled *Challenge and Effort: A Mindset Perspective*, at http://jffoster.wordpress.com/2013/09/07/ challenge-and-effort-a-mindset-perspective/. See also an article by Dona Matthews and Joanne Foster in the *Mindset Newsletter*, which can be found

at http://community.mindsetworks.com/blog-page/home-blogs/entry/mindsets-and-gifted-education-transformation-in-progress

141 Shaughnessy, 2010.

142 Metacognition can be applied directly to children's learning experiences. For example, children can select a book and monitor their own reading process as they go along by thinking about the material and making conscious connections with what they already know.

143 Del Siegle is a researcher and author whose work is well known in the field of gifted education. These four main considerations with respect to what makes something personally meaningful were noted in the course of a presentation he made at a SENG conference (Supporting Emotional Needs of Gifted), July 19, 2008 (Salt Lake City, Utah).

144 Dale Carnegie was an American author, perhaps most renowned for his best-selling book *How to Win Friends and Influence People*, 1936. Carnegie wrote about communication, self-confidence, and leadership, and he developed courses in self-improvement, corporate training, and interpersonal skills.

145 Foster, 2009, p. 490-491.

146 There is interesting information on bee bearding online (for starters, check out Wikipedia) including some pictures that kids might find intriguing—or possibly scary or gross. Of course, this is just an example of a topic that is suspenseful and controversial. A cautionary note—know your child's level of tolerance for words and pictures that may be powerful or upsetting before drawing their attention to this kind of material.

147 Kids use *boring* to mean several things: too easy, too hard, not interesting, intimidating, etc. Get to the root of what a child actually means by *boring*. Yet regrettably, many kids can't tell you.

148 Alfie Kohn in *The Myth of the Spoiled Child*, 2014, has some cautionary thoughts on rewards—the "do this and you'll get that" system can eventually have the effect of leaving kids focused on the "get that" more than on the "do this" and motivation never takes hold.

149 Thank you to the teacher candidates in my class, Foundations of Learning and Development—EDU3506, at the Ontario Institute for Studies in Education of the University of Toronto who generated impressive lists of motivators, some of which appear here. A total of 178 motivators was compiled in February, 2013, a list of 218 was generated in October, 2013, and 203 were shared in spirited discussion in October, 2014. Way to go!

150 Dona Matthews calls this the "just-right sweet spot of parenting" in her blog entitled *The Four Faces of "No": Finding the Just-Right Sweet Spot of Parenting*, posted on July 25th, 2013 at http://donamatthews.wordpress.com/2013/07/25/the-four-faces-of-no-finding-the-just-right-sweet-spot-of-parenting/.

151 An "attitude of abundance" is noted by Mark M. Maraia in his book *Relationships Are Everything: Growing Your Business One Relationship at a Time*, 2009. There are many business-oriented ideas that can be tweaked so as to inform parent-child relationships.

Chapter 12

152 In her book *Ain't Misbehavin'* (2009), Alyson Schafer advises parents to make a conscious effort to stop fighting with their children and to avoid using domination as a means of trying to control their behavior. On page 5, she writes, "Instead, we need to win their cooperation and help them find positive empowerment in their lives."

153 Bribery is a form of corruption with acquiescence as its end-goal. It is a trade-off that leads children to believe that if they comply, they will receive something as a result. It doesn't leave much room for self-regulation when a parent gives money or special consideration as a pay-off for what should be done anyhow.

154 Quotes from other celebrated people from various walks of life can be found within this book, including the following: JRR Tolkien; Margaret Mitchell; Anne Frank; William Jennings Bryan; Abraham Lincoln; Carol Dweck; Martin Luther King; J. M. Barrie; Calvin Coolidge; Malcolm Gladwell; Will Rogers; William James; Theodore Roosevelt; George Eliot; John F. Kennedy; Bill Gates; Walt Disney; Dale Carnegie; and William Shakespeare.

155 *Some of My Best Friends Are Books* by Judith Halsted, 2002, is a useful reference for parents and teachers looking for stories about protagonists with issues that children can relate to.

156 The *Phantom Tollbooth* by Norton Juster, 1961, is a story about a boy who embarks on a journey in his toy car and discovers The Lands Beyond. As Milo begins his magical adventure, he gets stuck in the Doldrums "where nothing ever happens and nothing ever changes" (p. 23) and he meets the Lethargarians—small creatures who spend their entire day dawdling, daydreaming, and dillydallying, except when they are lingering, loafing, and lounging. He meets the Watchdog who helps him think of ways to stop wasting time, and he encounters many other characters as he travels along and ultimately learns that life can be full of incredible excitement if he only takes initiative.

157 Young children might enjoy the story *Smelly Socks* by a bestselling team—author Robert Munsch and illustrator Michael Martchenko, 2004. The book is the tale of Tina, a girl who loves her brand new colorful socks and refuses to take them off—"Never!" she exclaims. The captivating storyline and lively illustrations provide a basis for discussion about what happens when a child procrastinates (in this case, not washing socks), and how such choices can affect others.

158 Emily Dickinson.

159 Dweck, 2006. According to Dweck, acquiring and sustaining a growth mindset is integral to learning and doing.

Index

About the Author

Joanne Foster, Ed.D., is co-author (with Dona Matthews) of *Beyond Intelligence: Secrets for Raising Happily Productive Kids* and the award-winning *Being Smart about Gifted Education*. As a parent, teacher, consultant, researcher, and education specialist, Dr. Foster has more than 30 years of experience working in the field of gifted education. She teaches at the Ontario Institute for Studies in Education at the University of Toronto. She presents on a wide range of topics at conferences and learning venues across North America, helping parents and educators support and encourage children's development. Dr. Foster also writes extensively, including "ABCs of Being Smart," a series of columns featured in the National Association for Gifted Children's journal *Parenting for High Potential*. Visit her website at www.beyondintelligence.net or contact her at joanne.foster@utoronto.ca.

CPSIA information can be obtained at www.ICGtesting.com
Printed in the USA
LVOW08s0613240115

424181LV00003B/3/P